Wade Fishing the Rapidan River of Virginia

From Smallmouth Bass to Trout

The Confluence to Skyline Drive

By Steve Moore

Published by Calibrated Consulting, Inc
ISBN: 978-0-9823962-9-2 (0-9823962-9-5)
Feedback: feedback@catchguide.com

Other CatchGuide books by Steve Moore:

Wade and Shoreline Fishing the Potomac River for Smallmouth Bass
Chain Bridge to Harpers Ferry

Trout and Smallmouth Fishing on the North Branch of the Potomac
A Western Maryland River

Steve Moore
The SwitchFisher- Bass or Trout... it's all good!
Fishing the Hazel River off Skyline Drive

Steve is an avid, hard-core, terminally addicted fisherman. He was ruined for life when his father introduced him to the sport at the age of 7 while living in Norway as a result of military duty. Chasing trout on mountain streams left an enduring imprint and drive to find new water... something that tortures Steve to this day.

Of course, this was preordained since Steve's father was fishing in a local bass tournament on the morning he was born. He claims to have had permission to go, but Steve's mother does not remember the actual facts matching that story. The point that he won a nice Shakespeare reel did nothing to mitigate the trouble he was in upon his return.

Dedication

This book is dedicated to Lon and his son, Sean, who have been my constant companions on both the Rapidan and Rappahannock. Even more gratitude goes to Lon's wife, Ann, who puts up with our expeditions and even supports them by driving the "Bass Taxi" to various drop points on the Rappahannock and the Rapidan. No matter where she dumps us, we seem to find our way out!

Hey Lon! You free? Water looks good!

Table of Contents

Introduction

This is the third book in the CatchGuide series and the fundamental theme remains the same. I wrote it to solve a basic problem that many of us share - we don't have a canoe or kayak or, if we do, we don't have ready access to a shuttle partner. Even if we did, canoe/kayak compatible launches on the Rapidan are widely spread and force a long day on the water. Some treks even require an overnight campout.

Therefore, this book focuses on wade fishing; that very physical style of angling that leverages shoe leather. I cover 18 access points and the adjacent 34 miles (approximate) of fishable river on the Rapidan between the confluence of the Rappahannock and its disappearance into a spring seep just below Skyline Drive high in the Blue Ridge Mountains.

Relying on foot power provides an angler a colossal advantage given the ebb and flow of the river during the summer. For example, a heavy burst of rain can fill the lower Rapidan with silt that blows out bass fishing for several days. That same rain energizes mountain trout and pitches them into a feeding frenzy as additional food surges into the narrow headwaters. Since the mountain streams run surprisingly clean and clear all year long, you are not "shut out" from fishing. Rather, change your target. Head up or downriver depending on the conditions.

Beyond flexibility, wading actually allows you to spend more time fishing the good spots. Once you start the long float down the river in a canoe or kayak, you are condemned to spend far more time than you like drifting over bad water or just paddling to get to the finish line. With the amount of water up or downstream from each of the access points limited only by your willingness to walk, you spend more time fishing the 10% of the water that holds 90% of the fish. Granted, a floating fisherman will be able to throw a lure in places that a wader can only dream about as a result of the barrier presented by distance and private property. But, in the long run, by following the guidance in this book, a wading angler will be able to spend more days on the river, in the right places, and have a better chance of catching a hungry, aggressive smallie or a feisty, colorful brook trout.

Finally, in a typical year, the Rapidan drops to a level by mid-June that will turn any kayak float into a very, very long hike requiring kayakers to drag their boats across numerous shallow stretches. So, you may as well wade and enjoy yourself. Need to know where? This is the book for you.

I certainly hope you find this CatchGuide helpful and wish you the best of luck on the stream.

Steve Moore

General Perspective on the Rapidan System

In an article he wrote for Eastern Fly Fishing magazine, my friend and fellow author, Beau Beasley (*Fly Fishing Virginia, Fly Fishing the Mid-Atlantic*), documented the history of the Rapidan River from a trout fishing perspective. In the article, I learned that the name of the river came from the combination of the words *rapid* and *Anne;* an unusual juxtaposition to honor Queen Anne of England who ruled from 1702 to 1714. In effect, the Rapidan became the Queens river. If you believe that this river is fit for a queen, you just underestimated the spectacular variety of fishing it offers. It's not fit for a queen; it's clearly fit for a king.

The best smallmouth bass fishing in the northeastern part of Virginia is centered on the confluence of the Rapidan and Rappahannock. This location is so well known and popular that if you mention the "confluence" to another angler, he will instantly know where you are talking about. What isn't well known is how to get there on foot. Most anglers experience that fisherman's playground by doing the long float downstream from either Kelly's Ford or the Rappahannock River Campground on the Rappahannock or Elys Ford on the Rapidan to the take-out at the Clore Brothers Outfitters near Fredericksburg. As I describe later, a short hike on an easy trail gives you the opportunity to fish this prime water.

Trout lie in wait, silent and sulking, in the tall mountains at the other end of the river. The Rapidan is one of the most famous rivers on the East Coast as a result of the carefully managed trout fishery in the Shenandoah National Park and the neighboring Rapidan Wildlife Management Area. Head to the mountains to hike and fish for miles from any of the access points discussed in this book. It's all catch and release, single hook and, thankfully, most people abide by that regulation; ensuring a vibrant population of fish in every pool.

Between those bookends, you have the typical mixed bag of good places, average places and places you shouldn't even think about going to ... not even once. Some spots start out bad, but if you are willing to walk in the river, I'll put you on some great fishing. Likewise, I'll do everything but go to the bridge crossing and post a sign saying "horrible fishing" to warn you away from the spots that are a total waste of time even though they are accessible.

In general, what makes water good for either species is structure; specifically, rocks and gravel. The farther downstream from the mountains the river runs, the sandier it gets. The good spots are those where a drop in elevation or a tight bend compresses the push of the water to purge the sand and reveal the bottom. If you were only to look at the river from bridge crossings, you would miss most of the good areas. As I fished the river, I resolved to try and wade at least a mile in either direction from each access point. In all but a few, I was successful in meeting that goal and, in the process, discovered those good spots that make up the magic 10% of the water holding 90% of the fish. The maps I include in the book provide a perspective on where those locations are so you can judge your physical ability to reach them. In addition, you may want to go beyond where I ended (or at least ended discussion for this book). It was not my intent to walk every mile of the river from the Confluence to Camp Hoover.

In addition to the 21 topographical maps, this book includes 162 GPS coordinates. Use that information to preview the river. The coordinates are in a format that is compatible with Google Maps and the ebook version of this volume actually has a hotlink that instantly opens the satellite view of that location. If you zoom in on a particular spot, you can assess the density of the rocks, the associated structure and make your own call in terms of whether that particular spot is "worth it." One caveat on the satellite picture. Google updates the satellite view periodically and it's the luck of the draw on the amount of intelligence you can gain. If the picture was taken at low water during the summer, you just hit a gold mine! At high resolution, you can see the rocks under the water and, if you look closely, the darker areas will show you where the deep water is and the big fish lie. When you stumble upon a low, clear water picture, print it out for future reference! As a purchaser of this book, the ebook is available from www.CatchGuides.com for only $7.95 using the discount code of "rapidan" while the offer lasts.

Beyond the GPS coordinates, review the 248 included pictures carefully. Like the coordinates, the staggering number of pictures allows you to cast an angler's eye on the water without having to burn the fossil fuel and even more precious human energy to reach that location. Use them to assess the shoreline structure and the character of the river. Between the satellite view and the pictures embedded in the book, you should know exactly what to expect before you put your foot on the gas pedal. My descriptions and advice round out the background. If you have the ebook, you should print the relevant chapter and take it with you as an "on water" reference.

I need to make three final comments:

- The first is that even though the Rapidan is generally shallow, there are deep sections that will surprise you; particularly if you fish when the water is milky. That demands you exercise the appropriate caution and wear a personal flotation device (PFD) to provide protection from any surprise the river offers up.
- The second is to point you back at the disclaimer and warning at the front of the book. You are ultimately accountable for what you do or fail to do on the river and I, the author, as well as the publisher and anyone else involved in the creation of this book disclaim all liability from actions you take. As stated in the disclaimer, by reading this book you agree to an unrestricted release from liability. If you cannot agree to that, then put this down right now and read something else.
- The GPS coordinates are shown in a format compatible with Google Maps. To load them into your GPS, remove the "minus" sign in front of the second number. Also, when you open Google Maps using the coordinates, *you may have to zoom out until you see the GREEN arrow*. Google tends to jump to a known feature - shown using a RED arrow.

Rules and Regulations

Where can you wade? Depends. And.... makes this the most difficult chapter of this book to write.

Sparks fly when the issue of river access comes up and the side of the argument you find yourself on usually depends on whether you own property that borders a waterway in the State. Even the professionals in the State government are reluctant to go on record with an opinion. So, now is the time to reiterate the opening disclaimer in the strongest of terms. I am not a lawyer, just a fisherman. This chapter contains my analysis of the situation that I coordinated with a number of different experts, who, for the same reason, have asked that nothing be attributed specifically back to them. **Nothing in this chapter should be regarded as legal advice**. The responsibility for any decision you make based on reading this, or, for that matter, using any information in this book, is yours alone and I point you back to the unrestricted release from liability disclaimer at the front of the book.

Trespassing

Before we get to the streambed, I need to cover the more general topic of trespassing. Other authors, in other books, sometimes refer to "informal" access points along the various rivers and streams in our State. Just because a road runs next to a stream does not mean you can walk from the roadway to the stream. In most cases, that thin strip of land separating the road from the water is privately owned. An exception is the Virginia Department of Transportation (VDOT) right-of-way. The right-of-way is a public easement that authorizes anyone to travel across the land included in the easement. In fact, many of the access points in this book properly use the VDOT right-of-way associated with bridges to get you to the water without problems. Here is how VDOT describes the right of way:

Definition: *"Right-of-way" means that property within the system of state highways that is open or may be opened for public travel or use or both in the Commonwealth. This definition includes those public rights-of-way in which the Commonwealth has a prescriptive easement for maintenance and public travel. The property includes the travel way and associated boundary lines, parking and recreation areas and other permanent easements for a specific purpose.* (24VAC30-151-10)

Note that the right-of-way can either be explicit with the strip of property owned by the State or it establishes a prescriptive easement that demands the property owner recognize the public's right to use the thin strip of his or her property that borders the road. I was pleased to see that the definition mentions both parking and recreation areas; confirming that we can leave our vehicles safely parked within the boundary of the easement. So, what's the formal definition of a road? According to the statute, ""Highway," "street," or "road" means a public way for purposes of vehicular travel, including the entire area within the right-of-way." Clearly, if the road is a State maintained road, the public has access to the entire area.

Size of the right-of-way: "*There is no standard right of way distance for every road. Generally, the right of way ranges from 25-150 feet from the road's center line.*" (VDOT website)

You have to talk to VDOT to determine the specific width of the right-of-way on the specific road in the specific place where you have questions. There may be some rare places when 25 feet will extend all the way to the water. If you believe you have discovered an instance where the river runs close enough to the road to be included in the right-of-way, you should discuss that with VDOT. To save you some work, I have already done the research for you regarding the Rapidan. I only found one place where there was a potential for the easement to overlap the streambed. Since this particular location was close enough to a bridge crossing where public rights are well-established, I did not bother to mention it in the discussion since a technical argument with a landowner will not end well at the edge of the river.

That establishes where you can be, but what if there are no "no trespassing" signs? How do you know who owns that strip of land? Unless you take the time to look it up on the Internet using the Graphical Information System (GIS) for your county (http://www.gispilot.com/States/Virginia.html), you should assume that it is private property. There are rare cases when state owned land extends from the water to the road and you can bet I documented every instance in this book. For example, the Hunting Run access point specifically uses the city and county owned property that borders the river on the north edge of the Hunting Run Reservoir. Likewise, there is public property at Elys Ford and other places that provide access to water not associated with a VDOT easement.

It's easy to use the GIS system. Do a generic search for the name of the county and the abbreviation, "GIS" or locate it on the summary site quoted above. Follow the instructions of the website to quickly zoom in on the actual property record and discover the name and address of the landowner. Using the name, do a look up in whitepages.com if you want to ask for permission to fish. If you would like to duplicate my research to convince yourself, the Rapidan runs adjacent to Stafford, Spotsylvania, Orange, Culpeper and Madison counties. In addition, Google Maps, at the most detailed resolution level, now shows property lines for many areas.

Here is how the Virginia (Section 18.2-119) defines the crime of trespassing:

"*If any person without authority of law goes upon or remains upon the lands, buildings or premises of another, or any portion or area thereof, after having been forbidden to do so, either orally or in writing... he shall be guilty of a Class 1 misdemeanor*"

Those of you who read words closely, have probably locked in on the phrase "*after having been forbidden to do so, either orally or in writing*"; immediately jumping to the conclusion that if there are no signs, then you can go anywhere you would like to go. Wrong.

Section 18.2-132 specifically targets hunters and fishers:

"Any person who goes on the lands, waters, ponds, boats or blinds of another to hunt, fish or trap without the consent of the landowner or his agent shall be deemed guilty of a Class 3 misdemeanor."

For the curious, a Class 3 misdemeanor will not only earn you a criminal record, but also inflict a fine of not more than $500 on you for your carelessness. Note that this section does not discuss whether notice was posted or not. Therefore, you need to exercise the appropriate care before you wander across property to get to the river. If it is private, and you are on it, whether it is posted or not, you are trespassing. Remember that thin strip of property I mentioned above? It counts.

One final critical point about permission. The best permission to have is written permission. If a conservation police officer stops you on posted land and you claim to have verbal permission from the landowner, he will likely ask you to prove it. Your word is not good enough and you will probably get a ticket that will be dropped later once you present proof from the landowner. I doubt that a call to the landowner on your cell phone would suffice. First of all, in many of the areas discussed, cell phone coverage is spotty. Second, how does the conservation police officer know that he is talking to the actual landowner? Therefore, the next time you see your landowner friend, have him sign a short, sweet and to the point permission slip that gives you the authority to use his property. Keep it with your fishing license.

VDOT Bridge Right-Of-Way

Given the uncertainties associated with whether the VDOT right-of-way extends from the road to the river, we must rely on the better known, and well established, easement that surrounds most bridge crossings in the State to reach the water's edge. The VDGIF is explicit about the public's right to use this access method. For example, when discussing access to the Rapidan river on its website, it states:

"Access may also be gained via several non established points. These consist of VDOT right-of-ways along bridges (e.g., Route 522 on the Rapidan)."

Therefore, as long as you stay within the right of way, you can skinny down the edge of the bridge to get to the river. Obviously, this is another area of contention if the landowner is not as educated as you are on what a VDOT right-of-way is. Of all the access points I discuss in the book, there are only two where this might be a problem. Given that the fishing is horrible at both, your potential opportunity to have a discussion evaporates. Unless you are a glutton for punishment, don't go to those two places.

Do not extrapolate this rule to every bridge in the State. Some bridges, especially those in the Shenandoah Valley, are privately owned and maintained. A State maintained road may not lead all the way to the bridge. If it's not a public road, there is no public right-of-way. All of the bridges discussed in this book are public with a public road running across them.

Streambed

So far, except for the key point about access near bridges, this chapter has been mostly bad news. What's a book on fishing doing spending so much time on where you cannot fish? It is important to stay legal. It is crucial to respect landowner rights or the situation worsens for all of us. If we do things to put the landowners adjacent to our State's waters up arms, we all lose since the issue of streambed ownership is not fully settled.

What many anglers do not understand is that the simple act of walking on the streambed triggers a whole new set of cautions. As a result of a dog's breakfast of conflicting rules including several hundred-year-old crown grants from the King of England, acts of the State Assembly and a limited set of court decisions carefully written to prevent broad application, Virginia does not make it easy to determine who owns the streambed on our State's waterways.

While the majority of the Rappahannock and Rapidan river systems are "good to go" in terms of public use and streambed access, there are some gray areas. While there are no access points discussed in this book that have been declared explicitly "off limits" based on the application of the exceptions to State ownership of the streambed, there is no clear, unequivocal regulation or decision that makes them on-limits either. Until that happens, you are on your own to make the call.

To understand the shade of gray, you need to understand a little bit of the legal situation.

Virginia's declaration that the State owns streambeds can be traced to the following statute first implemented in 1780:

Section 28.2-1200. Ungranted beds of bays, rivers, creeks and the shores of the sea to remain in common.

All the beds of the bays, rivers, creeks and the shores of the sea within the jurisdiction of the Commonwealth, not conveyed by special grant or compact according to law, shall remain the property of the Commonwealth and may be used as a common by all the people of the Commonwealth for the purpose of fishing, fowling, hunting...

While this established the State's ownership of streambeds and the right of the public to use them, the alert reader has probably already focused on the subtle phrase, "*not conveyed by special grant or compact*" That is where the argument starts. Given the age of Virginia and the inducements to colonization that existed prior to the American revolution, parts of the State were conveyed to individual landowners at some point in its early history.

Most anglers in Virginia are aware of the access issues associated with the Jackson River. In 1996, the Virginia Supreme Court recognized that "kings grants" issued by Kings George II and III in 1750 and 1759 respectively gave several landowners on the upper Jackson River some control over the river where it ran through their property. As a result of those grants, the Virginia statute did not apply ("*not conveyed by special grant*"), and the landowners owned the streambed as their personal property with the right to restrict access.

While the debate is settled on the specific, small section of the Jackson were a prior grant was established, there is no current debate on either the Rapidan or Rappahannock rivers as of 2010. Based on the explicit language of the statute quoted above, the public has access to the streambed as long as it obtains access legally – no trespassing. As of the date of publication, there are no known issues associated with the streambed on either river.

After waving the red flag for the last couple of paragraphs, there is a reasonable amount of clarity over portions of both the Rappahannock and the Rapidan.

In opinions tracing back to at least Bulletin 120 (*Public Recreation on Virginia's End and Streams: Legal Rights and Landowners Perceptions*), which was published in October 1979, there are references to a VDGIF position that the Rapidan is a public stream from its confluence at the Rappahannock to Raccoon Ford in Culpeper County. The comparable reference for the Rappahannock is from the mouth of the river to US Route 211 outside of Warrenton in Fauquier County. There should be no question about any access downstream of these two locations.

In addition, there was a State act regarding the Rappahannock that extends the navigation from the "*... most convenient place on tide water upwards to the highest parts practicable on the main branch and other branches thereof....*" It provided that "*... the said river and the branches thereof, and the works to be erected thereon in virtue of this act, when completed, shall forever thereafter, be esteemed and taken to be navigable as a public highway....*" another proof point that confirms that the State regards both rivers as navigable and the beds remain the property of the Commonwealth.

Therefore, for the Rapidan, the "gray" area is anything above Raccoon Ford and below the Graves Mill entrance at the Shenandoah National Park. However, I believe that it is not actually a gray area at all. All you need to is look at the deep tire tracks on the dirt roads that hug tight inside the VDOT easement leading to small parking areas underneath or adjacent to the bridges. On any given weekend in the summer, you will not be alone at any of these locations. The majority of them are long established and well used fishing and swimming holes for the local residents. Finally, the reference on the VDGIF website regarding using the VDOT bridge easements discusses a bridge above Raccoon Ford; confirming that the actual, firmly public, area goes farther upstream beyond what was stated in Bulletin 120.

That said, the bridge crossings on Route 622 and Wolftown Road are the most vulnerable to selective interpretation regarding public access given the width of the stream at those points. I'm not really sure the width or depth matters given the first line of the statute, "*All the beds of the bays, rivers, creeks...*" These spots are routinely used as canoe put-in and take-out points. If you are interested in fishing those locations, read my description closely and you should conclude that the right choice is to pass on the opportunity since the fishing is nonexistent.

There is a bottom line in the above discussion. As anglers, and we need to respect the rights of landowners and not violate private property. Even though, right now, we can use the streambed without restriction, recognize that the shoreline for most of the length of the river is privately owned. When wading in the river, chances are you will eventually get to a place where the water is too deep to allow you to continue. If you exit the river without returning to the legal access point, you are probably trespassing on private property.

Water Volume and Flow

Knowledge of current river conditions will save you a significant amount of frustration and heartache. The quality of the fishing comes and goes with both the amount and clarity of the water. If you know what to look for and where to check to determine the current conditions, you will avoid wasted treks in grinding traffic only to discover an unfishable situation. USGS maintains two gages (yes, they spell it "gage" instead of "gauge") to monitor the status on the Rapidan river. One is near Ruckersville and the other is farther downstream at Culpeper. Neither are useful for the trout section of the river since the ebb and flow in the mountains depends more on rainfall than accumulated runoff. To keep things simple, I base my assessments on the Culpeper gage.

As a general statement, to be wadeable, the flow must be far below the minimum level to make whitewater addicts happy. There is a great website – www.americanwhitewater.org – the kayak crowd uses to determine put-in and take-out points and share conditions. If you use a kayak or canoe, I strongly encourage you to join by going to their website. The website has real-time river flow status color-coded based on a kayaker's point of view for different sections of the river:

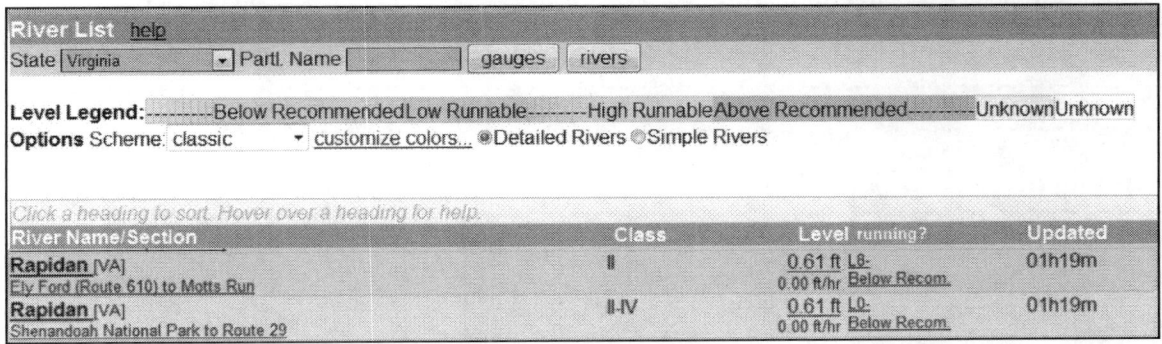

When you click on an entry, the website provides expanded guidance on minimum/maximum whitewater levels. The gage height range that would make the trip worthwhile for a kayaker is between 1.6 and 18.0 feet (if you have a death wish...) on the lower Rapidan and 4.0 to 6.0 feet on the upper section. if you are going to wade fish on the Rapidan, even the minimum level is far above what I consider to be the maximum safe level. Therefore, all this tells you is whether you will be bothered by kayakers when you are fishing. If it's below the recommended minimum, chances are that people will not embark on the float downstream.

So what is the number for wade fishing? Frankly, I used to base my judgment on the gage height and used the general rule that the Rapidan was wadeable at a gage reading of 1.41 or below. As I did the coordination for this book, I discovered that gage height is a poor measurement. The USGS told me that gage height is an arbitrary reading and is only used to calculate discharge. Since the river channel is dynamic and constantly changing, they correct the gage height to match current conditions. As they assess the situation, they may determine a significant change has occurred and develop a new gage height standard. Therefore, the only reliable statistic is discharge in cubic feet per second. I have not had problems wading in some places in the Rapidan at readings of 600 CFS and below with the best conditions being under 200 cfs. Unlike the North Branch of the Potomac where there is consensus and collective wisdom associated with safe wading levels attached to cubic feet per second, there is no similar body of knowledge for the Rapidan. So, use my experience as a yardstick and, as you fish the river, make your own judgments. In the pictures associated with each access point, I usually document the discharge volume associated with that visit. You can throw your eyeball on the picture, assess the water and decide.

Another interesting dynamic is that it appears the discharge in the Rapidan has decreased over the years. I show two tables at the back of the book. One is based on the full 78 year record and the other is based on nine years between 2000 and 2009. If you subtract one from the other, you discover the surprising statistic that, except for September, November and December, the river has been running significantly lower than historical averages would dictate.

The table below shows the monthly average difference. I know this tracks with my recent experience since it seems like the end of August is always a pretty tough time to fish the river unless you go to Hunting Run or the US 29 bridge where there always seems to be plenty of deep water and good fishing.

Difference in Average CFS (78 year average - 9 year average)											
Jan	Feb	Mar	Apr	May	Jun	Jul	Aug	Sep	Oct	Nov	Dec
-148	-134	-154	-74	-56	-44	-22	-130	114	-72	71	64

The bottom line is that there is always someplace to fish on this river; even at low levels. Pay attention to the descriptions of each access point and look for places where there is deeper water.

In addition to making sure the discharge volume is at the appropriate level matched to your physical capability before going out, you must consider recent rainfall. The bass section of the Rapidan is silty. A small amount of rain will push huge volumes of mud into the river. Since it seems that the Rapidan does not flow as fast as the Rappahannock, it takes much longer for the Rapidan to clear up. Therefore, you should be prepared to shift over to the Rappahannock if the conditions on the Rapidan are bad when you arrive. A rule of thumb is that it takes at least three days for the silt to drop out of the water.

This does not apply to the trout water in the mountains. While a huge rain may throw some milk in the mountain streams, it disappears quickly. During the appropriate season, trout can always be an alternative to bass if you are intent on fishing the Rapidan.

Best Time to Fish

The Rapidan is fishable 365 days of the year. Since it has both trout and bass, there is always something moving regardless of the season.

Trout

To narrow the window down a bit, the prime season for brook trout is in the spring between February and May. By the time June rolls around, you need to pay attention to the water temperature to ensure that it is below 65°. Above that level, catching a fish may stress it to the point of mortality. In no case should you fish in the mountains once the temperature pokes above 70°.

The temperatures in the Fall quickly dip below the 65° mark and solve the warmth problem, but there is a new challenge. The Fall is when brook trout spawn. They do this by creating nests (called redds) within the sand and gravel beds tucked in the nooks and crannies of the stream. A careless angler can wipe out an entire generation of a brook trout family by stepping in the water in the wrong place. For this reason, many avoid fishing once the spawn starts in October. If you resolve not to step in the water and are careful to avoid getting wet, you can still fish during this time of year. Use your judgment. One way to ensure you maintain focus on the problem is to not wear waders. The shock of ice cold water will be a reminder to be careful.

As the season turns to winter, the water temperature drops to the point where many fish become inactive. A fishing trip into the mountains when the water temperature is below 40° is mostly a cold, miserable hike . Granted, my perspective is colored by years in wretched places when I was in the Army. At minimum, you will get fresh air!

Unfortunately, there is no gage close enough to the mountains to give a constant readout of water temperature. Even though it is too far away from the mountains to be exact, the historical data indicate that the water drops below the 40° threshold in mid-January and persists through February. Since the Culpeper gage measured the temperature a considerable distance from the mountains, subtract a few degrees and you should be within the ballpark. For more exact numbers, you need to rely on input from other anglers obtained on various fishing websites or by participating in trout oriented forums. I do not recommend using the limited historical data available for the gage to judge spring and summer temperatures since the water in the mountains is shielded from the hot Virginia sun that warms it by the time it reaches the Culpeper gage.

Bass

Unlike trout, bass are pretty tough critters. When to fish for bass is driven more by the water level than by temperature. Since there is no active temperature gage on either the Rapidan or Rappahannock, I use the Potomac as a surrogate. The Little Falls gage still provides temperature readings that correlate loosely with what you can expect on the Rapidan. Once the temperature reading inches above 50°, the threshold for spawning, I start to get interested in the water levels.

From a temperature perspective, a Rapidan smallmouth starts to move in mid-March, but the water volume usually remains above 600 cfs until late April; depending on the intensity of the Spring rains. Don't be fooled. The Rapidan can surge to 12 feet or more; becoming life-threatening very quickly. In addition, with all of the Spring rain, you can count on the Rapidan to remain clouded until the intensity and frequency of the storms abate. As with any smallmouth river, there is a significant danger in wading when you cannot see the bottom. Since the water is cold, you will undoubtedly wear chest waders that increase your opportunity to drown as a result of a careless step into a deep hole. If you decide to abandon the trout to go for early season smallmouth, be sure you wear a PFD!

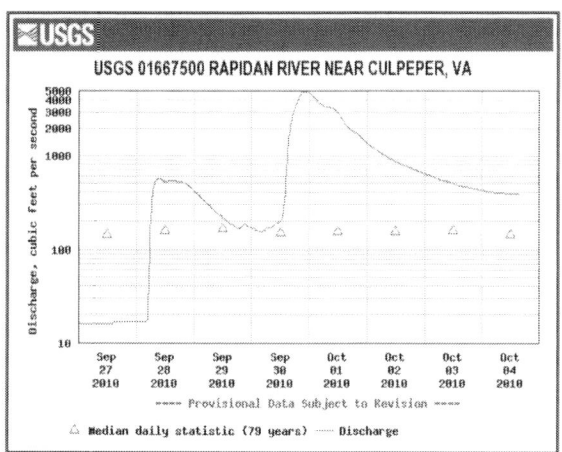 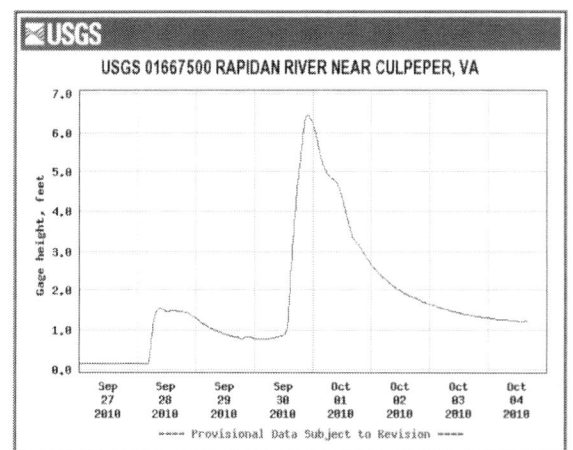

On this single day, the river rose from 20 cfs to just under 600 cfs and then jumped to almost 5000 two days later!

If you use gage height as your criteria, check this out. It jumped from under one foot to over six feet in one day! Be careful and be aware!

On the good news front, since March, April and May are in the middle of trout season, there are few anglers working the lower river during those months. Those who do are usually kayakers or canoeists who take advantage of the high water to make the run from Elys Ford to the Clore Brothers landing. The result is that you should have plenty of solitude at many of the locations discussed in this book. Given the distance between put-in and take-out, floating fisherman rarely have the opportunity to dwell long in a single place.

Your first opportunity to wet wade will not be until the middle to the end of May when the water temperature punches through the 70° mark - but it doesn't really get comfortable until mid-June when it claws up towards 80°. At the other end of the calendar, the action dies off in mid-October when the temperature dips below 60°. Joyfully, this correlates perfectly with the restart of trout season. If you want to avoid disturbing the mountain trout, Virginia, Maryland and West Virginia all begin their fall stocking programs in mid-October. Good stocked trout water near the Rapidan includes the Rose, Robinson and Hughes Rivers. So, there is always a fish to catch!

Once you rationalize the water temperature, recognize that the gage reading shown in Culpeper is a rough measurement when applied across the entire river. The specific level at the various access points is driven by the physical geography at that particular place. Therefore, where the river is wide, the depth and associated impact of the water volume will be less (easier to wade) and vice versa.

All that goes to say that the best time for smallmouth fishing is between early June and late September.

Understanding the Rating System

Every angler looks at a body of water in a way that matches his background and compares what he sees to his personal concept of "perfect." I am no different. To fully understand the comments I make in this guide, you need to understand how I evaluate water.

The tables below attempt to normalize my perspective into a common frame of reference. The key ratings are the ones related to physical fitness, the wadeability of a particular stretch, and whether spin or fly gear provides the right technical approach to catch more fish - or even whether it is feasible to fly fish at all.

The one rating that I do not include is whether fishing a particular section is dangerous. While I will point out the hazards that were apparent to me, for obvious reasons associated with liability, *you must be the final arbiter on whether you are comfortable fishing in a particular location and must use your common sense based on the conditions on that particular day prior to entering the water. You are solely and fully responsible for any decision you make to enter the river.*

The physical fitness rating is based on my impression of what it takes to get to the fishing area and enjoy it. Something I consider challenging may be easy for you or, on the other end of the scale, impossible based on your personal physical situation. *You should never attempt to fish in any spot where taking a step off the bank creates personal risk*. Just because I did not think a particular place was overly taxing physically may not mean much until you match your abilities with mine.

Please re-read and agree to the liability disclaimer at the front of the CatchGuide before you read further.

The tables below lay out the criteria:

Rating Explanations		
Parking	**Green**	Formal parking area with plenty of spaces
	Yellow	Informal parking area off the main road
	Red	Park on the side of the road
Canoe or Kayak Launch	**Green**	Access point useable by canoes or kayaks; short portage from the parking area
	Yellow	Useable but requires a carry
	Red	No easy access to launch a canoe or kayak - long walk or no path
Distance to River	**Green**	Parking area is next to the river
	Yellow	Short walk of less than 1/2 mile
	Red	Walk of more than 1/2 mile
Can Bike to River	**Green**	Using a bike would be useful and is permitted
	Red	Bike not permitted or not useful
Physical Fitness	**Green**	Smooth flow, easy wading, stable bottom
	Yellow	Some rock ledges, moderate water speed
	Red	Caution - fast water, slippery rocks or both
Scenery	**Green**	Steep cliffs, riffles, or grass beds
	Yellow	Flat water, broad sweep of river
	Red	Populated

Rating Explanations

Spin Fishing	Green	No problems using spin gear
	Yellow	Structure may cause hang ups
	Red	Water limits use of spin gear (short shallow pools, etc)
Fly Fishing	Green	Open terrain allows backcast
	Yellow	Some obstructions for backcast
	Red	Tight vegetation; No room for backcast
Trout	Green	Trout are present
	Red	Trout are not present
Bass	Green	Bass are present
	Red	Bass are not present
Pressure	Green	Likely to see few other people
	Yellow	Will see other people, but will not feel pressured
	Red	Very popular location; typically crowded
Overall	Green	Always a good choice
	Yellow	A good choice if you do not have anywhere better to go
	Red	Not worth the time or the gas

Overall Rating Summary

The following two tables consolidate all of the ratings in one place for your reference.

	Parking	Boat Launch	Distance to River	Can Bike to River	Physical Fitness	Scenery
The Confluence	Red	Red	Red	Green	Red	Green
Hunting Run	Yellow	Red	Red	Green	Yellow	Green
Elys Ford	Green	Green	Green	Red	Green	Yellow
Germanna	Red	Yellow	Yellow	Red	Yellow	Green
Raccoon Ford	Green	Yellow	Yellow	Red	Green	Yellow
Route 522 Bridge	Yellow	Green	Green	Red	Green	Yellow
Rapidan Dam	Yellow	Green	Green	Red	Green	Red
Madison Mills	Green	Green	Green	Red	Green	Green
Liberty Mills	Red	Yellow	Green	Red	Green	Yellow
US 29	Yellow	Green	Green	Red	Yellow	Green
Wolftown Road	Red	Red	Yellow	Red	Yellow	Green
Graves Mill (662)	Red	Red	Yellow	Red	Red	Green
Graves Mill (SNP)	Green	Green	Green	Red	Red	Green
Staunton River	Green	Red	Red	Red	Red	Green
Quaker Run	Yellow	Green	Green	Red	Red	Green
1st Bridge	Red	Red	Yellow	Red	Red	Green
2nd Bridge	Red	Red	Yellow	Red	Red	Green
Camp Hoover	Red	Red	Red	Red	Red	Green

Here are the remaining ratings and an overall summary assessment for each location:

	Spin Fishing	Fly Fishing	Trout	Bass	Pressure	Overall
The Confluence	Green	Green	Red	Green	Yellow	Green
Hunting Run	Green	Green	Red	Green	Green	Green
Elys Ford	Green	Green	Red	Green	Yellow	Green
Germanna	Green	Green	Red	Green	Yellow	Green
Raccoon Ford	Green	Green	Red	Green	Green	Red
Route 522 Bridge	Green	Green	Red	Green	Green	Yellow
Rapidan Dam	Green	Green	Red	Green	Yellow	Yellow
Madison Mills	Green	Green	Red	Green	Green	Green
Liberty Mills	Green	Green	Red	Green	Yellow	Red
US 29	Green	Green	Red	Green	Yellow	Green
Wolftown Road	Green	Green	Red	Red	Green	Red
Graves Mill (662)	Green	Green	Red	Red	Green	Red
Graves Mill (SNP)	Green	Green	Green	Red	Red	Yellow
Staunton River	Red	Red	Green	Red	Green	Green
Quaker Run	Green	Green	Green	Red	Red	Yellow
1st Bridge	Green	Green	Green	Red	Red	Yellow
2nd Bridge	Red	Yellow	Green	Red	Green	Green
Camp Hoover	Red	Red	Green	Red	Green	Red

The Confluence

Google Map Coordinates: 38.36767,-77.618022

Summary Rating

Parking	Red	Spin Fishing	Green
Canoe/Kayak Launch	Red	Fly Fishing	Green
Distance to River	Red	Trout	Red
Can Bike to River	Green	Smallmouth Bass	Green
Physical Fitness	Red	Pressure	Yellow
Scenery	Green	Overall	Green

There is no better fishing location for smallmouth bass in Virginia than the confluence of the Rapidan and the Rappahannock. All of the "red" ratings are actually positive factors that contribute to reducing the pressure. Most of the other anglers in the confluence float to this location on a canoe or a kayak. For those without a boat, the one mile walk down the moderate hill to reach the river filters out much of the other potential pressure.

Special Regulations

There are no special fishing regulations in effect at this location.

Getting to the Stream

From I-95, merge onto VA 3 west at Fredericksburg and follow it for just under 9 miles. Turn right on Elys Ford Road (VA 610), go across the Rapidan and continue 4 miles. Turn right on Richards Ferry Road (VA 619) and follow it to the end. A thousand feet before you get to the end, the road will split. Take the right hand fork. Park on the right hand side of the road at the end (38.382053,-77.625339). There are "no parking" signs on the opposite side to keep it clear so there will be room to turn around and get out.

At the end of the cul-de-sac, go past the gate on the City of Fredericksburg trail that leads to their campsite on the river (38.374871,-77.619481). Immediately prior to the campsite, the trail lurches right to move downstream. Take that fork and walk another 0.5 mile to get to the Confluence. The trail ends at the campsite that sits in at the junction of the two rivers (38.368276,-77.619395).

Canoe/Kayak Comment: There is no launch point within a reasonable distance of the river. From the parking area at the end of Richards Ferry Road, it is a half mile to the river. Likewise, there is no take-out at the confluence itself. The closest put-in is at the Rappahannock River Campground and the next take-out is at the Clore Brothers parking lot.

Environment and Fish

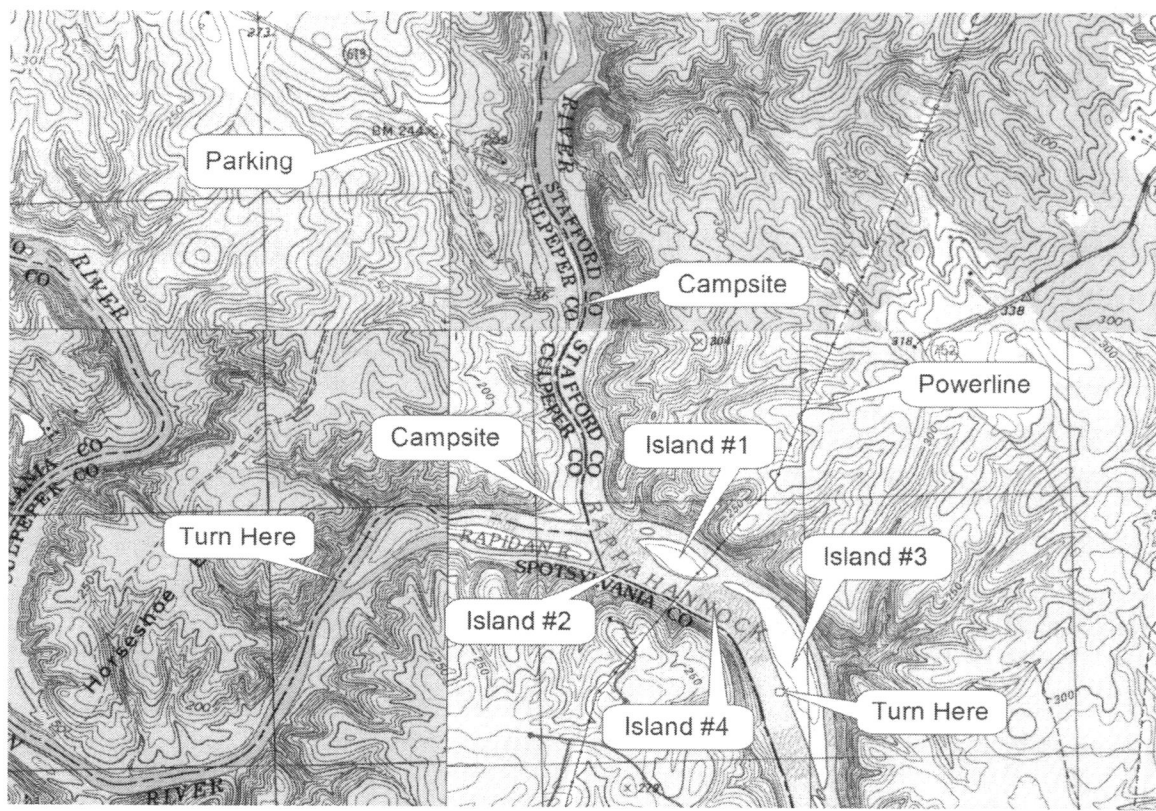

Without a doubt, the Confluence is the best place to fish for smallmouth bass in the entire Rappahannock and Rapidan River network. The Confluence is a jumble of boulders, slick ledges, channels and pools that conspire to create the perfect habitat for smallmouth and the ideal fishing destination for anyone willing to make the walk to the junction or float a kayak or canoe from Elys Ford.

The trail from the parking area is an easy downhill walk and not a bad climb on the way back out. It will be an exercise in self-discipline to ignore the roar of the Rappahannock on the left as you keep your sights focused on the ultimate goal. However, as soon as you reach the tip of land (38.368276,-77.619395) that marks the junction between the two rivers and can gaze upstream at the Rappahannock on the left or the Rapidan to the right, as well as absorb the panorama of jumbled structure downstream where the two rivers crash together, whatever sweat it cost to get here is instantly worth it.

In fact, you may have a nervous breakdown on the spot generated by an overwhelming wave of uncertainty about where to start. You are truly the kid in a candy store with a pocket full of cash and everything on sale. It's just that good!

All of the water downstream of where you stand is in the Rappahannock. There are actually two sections of the Confluence - the one just in front of you and the "lower Confluence" that starts three quarters of a mile downstream (38.360638,-77.610319). Since the lower section is completely within the Rappahannock system, I defer discussion of it to my book, *Wade Fishing the Rappahannock River of Virginia*. In addition, that book contains the detailed discussion of the section of the Rappahannock from the Confluence upstream to where the trail joins the river.

That said, you have days of fishing spread out in front of you. To completely exploit the Confluence will take several trips. The best way to deal with it is to execute a search pattern that starts on the right running in parallel bands starting from north to south. The reason to start to the right is simple. As you look left, there is a side channel separated from the northern shoreline by a large, grassy island (38.367031,-77.615962 - Island #1). Up until the end of July, plenty of water fills the channel and it creates a "mini-river" all by itself. Since it is narrow, the best approach is to head upstream. Therefore, leave that section to the end of the day as you work back up to the trailhead to hike back to your vehicle.

Start fishing in the deep pools to the left as you enter the river from the tip of the campsite. Fish carefully because earlier in the year large smallmouth congregate near the campsite. It is after the campsite has been visited repeatedly by canoeists and kayakers making the overnight voyage down to Fredericksburg that these fish wise up and go elsewhere. As soon as you step off the bank, you find yourself in a wide open area marked by small tufts of grass clinging to the tops of a convoluted jumble of dense boulder structure that represents a nightmare to boaters as they try and work their way through the junction. Their agony is your joy as each represents a channel leading to a pool and every pool holds fish. Granted, you can catch sunfish anywhere you throw a lure in the Confluence. These feisty fish will aggressively attack anything that is small enough to get into their mouths. Therefore, you should upsize your terminal tackle unless you actually want to catch them.

If you are hunting for a larger fish, focus on pools that are least 3 feet deep. At the start of the season, the big boys penetrate into the shallower water, but at the height of summer they move to the deeper pools or rest in the shade along the shoreline.

Once you fish the area in the immediate vicinity of the tip, point your rod south and fish across the mouth of the Rapidan to the southern shoreline. There's a large blowdown of jumbled logs that shelter some deep water that should get your attention. As you fish your way around it, it should also be a lesson to you regarding the power of the river at full flood. The massive fallen tree that forms the base of the jumble did not grow and eventually die in that spot. The river pushed it from upstream when the river was at high flow. It is a visible example of why you must pay close attention to the gage reading to ensure that you are not about to step into a torrent of water and risk death by drowning.

Once past the blowdown, look downstream to the small island (38.366745,-77.617282 - Island #2) that divides the river into two sections. Island #1 is to the left, the shoreline is to the right with a narrow channel running around the right side of Island #2. Fish your way to Island #2 and continue down the southern channel between it and the shore. Eventually, you will see the old rock wall of the canal where the river picks up some speed as it grinds against the shoreline. There are some good pools over on that side and you should fish those as you work all the way down to the slack water that occurs upstream of the power lines (38.365481,-77.615372). The power lines represent a critical boundary. They are about 500 yards downstream of the campsite. If you continue farther downstream, you will have a longer, tougher walk back to your vehicle. Therefore, if you feel tired, fish up the southern side of Island #1 or walk to the other side and fish the tight channel that embraces the northern shoreline to complete your search pattern.

If you fish up the south side of Island #1, stay to the middle of the channel between it and Island #2 (38.366745,-77.617282). That area holds the deepest water and the possibility of larger fish. If the flow is good enough, and you decide to go to the other side of Island #1, do not start fishing upstream immediately from the downstream tip of the island. Instead, walk another 200 yards downstream to the tip of yet another, even larger island (38.364104,-77.610555 - Island #3) that compresses the side channel into a narrow band about 30 feet wide. The reason is that the 200 yards you would have skipped is a maze of "deeper" 2 to 3 foot holes with channels leading into them. From the tip of Island #3, fish your way upstream targeting the northern shoreline. You can easily pick up 20 fish in this section floating poppers against the rocks and over the channels.

Once you work the 200 yard section, continue up the northern shoreline where the river narrows and pools at the base of three distinct gradient breaks (one is at the power line, the next is 150 feet upstream and the final is at the tip of the island). Each represents an opportunity to catch a larger fish. After fishing the first two breaks moving upstream, there is a narrow band of trees separating Island #1 from the northern shoreline. At lower water, you can flip a coin to decide which side to fish, but I prefer the northern side because it is wider and offers deeper pools. At the upstream tip of the island, there is a large, obvious ridge of rocks that separates this entire geographic structure from the main part of the river. Fish the pools and return to the campsite.

Early morning fog shrouds the confluence looking upstream to the junction.

View downstream towards the junction from the Rapidan at 119 CFS.

View upstream - Island #2 is to the right. River running at 638 cfs.

This is the confluence at its finest. The numerous grass islands, channels and rocks all work together to create the optimum smallmouth bass environment.

Another view of the great structure in the confluence looking upstream towards the junction from the power line.

Be prepared to catch massive smallmouth at the confluence. This guy (21") hit a small blue popper floated next to log near island #3.

Power Line Downstream

If you have the energy, you may want to walk directly to the power line and start fishing there. Your target for the day is the section of rapids immediately downstream of the power line and the western shore of Island #3 at river left. The river is deepest in the vicinity of the power line. Fish either side of the small island (38.365567,-77.613859 - Island #4) that is the key terrain feature breaking the river into two sections upstream of Island #3. Looking downstream at the bottom of Island #4, the part of the river between it and Island #3 is mostly shallow. Continue to fish downstream on river right until abreast of the tip of Island #3. At that point, walk over to Island #3 and fish its western shoreline. After experiencing the great water between Island #1 and the northern shoreline, you might assume the character of the river would be similar between Island #3 and the shoreline. Don't bother. The river goes slack and the bottom turns into sand. If you poke your nose in that direction, you will have a 500 yard walk with nothing to show for it. That said, I have had friends find some decent fish there. I write that off to luck and confused fish taking a wrong turn.

The bottom of Island #3 marks the boundary of what I consider to be the Confluence. The Rappahannock book will talk about the next stretch - the lower Confluence.

This is the view downstream looking towards island #3 from the power line.

Midway alongside island #3 facing downstream at 638 cfs.

This is the view upstream at the gap between island #1 and #3. The deep channel is on the right near the shore.

Downstream into the gap between island #3 and the shoreline. Do not fish beyond the gap since the river gets shallow and sandy. Concentrate on the water from the tip of island #3 upstream.

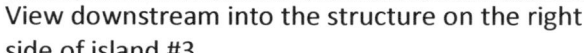

View downstream into the structure on the right   Upstream towards the power line from island #3.
side of island #3.

Rapidan Upstream

After all this discussion, maybe I should talk about the actual Rapidan! First of all, if you walk into the Confluence, don't bother to fish upstream into the Rapidan until after you have fully explored the area immediately downstream of the junction. In either direction -- whether you go upstream on the Rapidan or the Rappahannock -- the fishing will not be as good as it is in the actual Confluence. That said, you will encounter superb smallmouth habitat and fishing on the first leg of the Rapidan.

When you step off the shoreline at the campsite at the tip of the Confluence, the terrain on the southern shore is not actually the main shoreline. Instead, it's a long island that is approximately 1,000 yards long. There is a thin strip of the Rapidan River separating it from the actual shoreline. I have to admit that I have not fished that narrow stretch of water and leave it to you to discover or a future update to this book to describe. On the times that I visited, there did not seem to be enough water moving out of the downstream end of the island complex to make it interesting so I always deferred to the main stem of the river pushing around the northern perimeter. If you make the same decision, you will not be disappointed.

The large blowdown described earlier forms the lower boundary of the Rapidan River. Clearly, you should fish the lower boundary and its environs thoroughly as you begin your journey upstream. The next 600 yards will be consistently good. The river widens out with fewer rock outcroppings poking above the surface of the water. However, that does not mean there are not channels and fish. As you fish upstream, target the areas that appear to be a darker shade of green. That's the dead giveaway of deeper water that holds the larger fish. Fish both sides of any boulders that break above the surface as they typically form the boundary of a channel.

200 yards upstream from the mouth of the river, there is an island complex at 38.368074,-77.621906. The river has thrown a substantial number of logs and brush against the upstream side of the two islands that form the anchor points of the complex. As a result, there are deeper channels at the edges where the river has had to grind its way around the blockage. Be sure you spend an appropriate amount of time in this particular area to leverage the prime real estate.

Upstream, the next hundred yards offer up deeper water that will push you to either shore in order to move upstream with two noticeably deep pools occurring at 38.368324,-77.623775 and 38.368247,-77.624947. The second splays out in an interesting circular pattern that allows you to move on the rock ledges and fish it from all angles to include the narrow, fast channel that moves along the northern shoreline of the river. Just upstream of this point, there is a beach (38.368375,-77.62583) that kayakers use as a breakpoint on their journey downstream. Surprisingly, the popularity of that campsite has not impacted the fishing. Catch and release works!

Around the bend from the campsite, the river slows and broadens; becoming deeper on the southern shore. Depending on the water level, you may have some challenges working your way through and should stick to the northern shoreline where the water is most shallow. The next good fishing opportunity is at the three parallel rock ridges that start at 38.368116,-77.628214. Fish up and downstream of each ridgeline, but do not ignore the center where the water color darkens over the deep water.

View upstream into the Rapidan from the mouth of the confluence.

The beach and the campground are in the background of this picture at 38.368375,-77.62583. The stretch of water that leads through the rocky channels is all good.

This logjam sits at the entrance to the Rapidan. Be sure and fish the deep section to the right.

Note the mixed grass/sand/rock structure on the bottom.

This is where the river begins to broaden. It gets deep around the corner.

This is the deep "lake" in the vicinity of 38.36469,-77.630478.

At the lake, spin fishermen have the advantage as a result of the depth of the water that pushes you to the shore; limiting the opportunity for fly rodders to deploy an effective, long-range backcast. Be prepared to fish deep in this location. Even at only 40 CFS, it was hard to get around on the right-hand bank.

Bottom Line

Although I just attempted to do it, words cannot describe the Confluence. While there is good fishing elsewhere on the Rapidan River, the Confluence represents a model of perfection that cannot be duplicated.

Hunting Run

Google Map Coordinates: 38.354749,-77.641776

Summary Rating

Parking	Yellow	Spin Fishing	Green
Canoe/Kayak Launch	Red	Fly Fishing	Green
Distance to River	Red	Trout	Red
Can Bike to River	Green	Smallmouth Bass	Green
Physical Fitness	Yellow	Pressure	Green
Scenery	Green	Overall	Green

The combination of the 0.7 mile hike down the Hunting Run Trail, combined with the requirement to do a minimal amount of bushwhacking and slide down a steep bank to reach the river's edge, limits the pressure on this location. You can mitigate the physical impact of the short hike by using a bike to bump your way along the rutted trail to the river's edge. The deep water, broad ledges and rocky structure supporting the scattered grass islands makes this a good spot to fish. In fact, all things considered, Hunting Run almost offers up "confluence equivalent" fishing.

Special Regulations

There are no special fishing regulations in effect at this location.

Getting to the Stream

From I-95, take exit 130B onto VA 3 W (Plank Rd) toward Culpeper. Turn right on VA 620 (Spotswood Furnace Road) and follow it for 6 miles. Be alert once you cross over the stream that exits out of Hunting Run Reservoir on the left. Drive slowly up the hill until you see the unnamed road that pushes between some tall trees leading to an iron bar gate. You can see the gate from VA 620. Park to the right of the gate.

Canoe/Kayak Comment: It is a very long walk to drop a boat into the water; requiring a carry of 0.7 miles including maneuvering around a few obstacles on the trail.

Environment and Fish

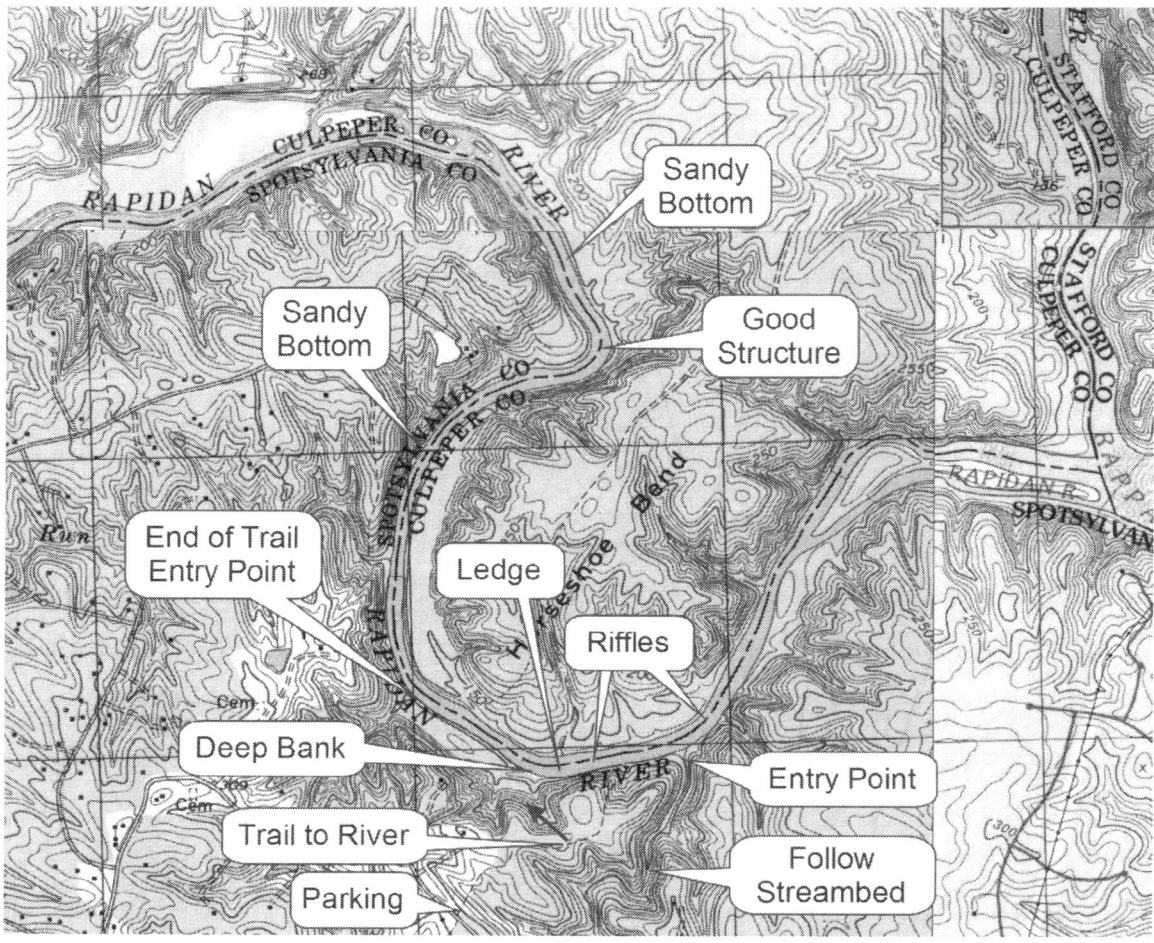

Once you park, there are two options to reach the river and whether you want to fish upstream or down dictates your choice. If you decide to go upstream, it is a relatively easy walk to reach the river. Downstream brings an entirely new set of problems and challenges. Both options get you to good water. The common problem you face is how to avoid trespassing near the building at the end of the road.

In most other places in this book, I break the experience into an "upstream" or "downstream" context. While you can go upstream or downstream, the best fishing experience is to do a little of both. Therefore, while I provide an upstream or downstream context, I'll start with the recommended strategy.

Recommended Mix

Walk down the smooth gravel road beyond the gate. Look for the marked entrance to Hunting Run Trail 0.2 miles from the gate on the left at 38.35657,-77.63893. While initially steep as it moves down the hill, it is only a half mile to reach the river. In fact, this is a perfect place to use a bike. Not only is the road beyond the gate wide and level, the trail is typically 3 feet wide and mostly flat with only a few deep ruts and downed trees to negotiate. There are a few places where you have to get off the bike and walk around an obstacle. Since it is all downhill to the flat plain that parallels the river, you can cruise quickly to the start of your day of fishing.

Just to provide a complete description, if you ignore Hunting Run Trail and continue down the road, you will encounter a "No Trespassing" sign posted on a tree when you are within sight of the County building at the edge of the river. Obviously, this is as far as you can go without violating the law. The river is temptingly close on the other side of the building and you can hear its siren song as it roars past. You have the opportunity to make three bad choices here.

The first is to ignore the sign, walk directly to the building and violate the law -- clearly, this is the worst choice. I strongly recommend you not take this option. Besides, having waded downstream from the correct access point upriver, the bank that supports the building is steep and well protected by poison ivy and sticker bushes that conspire to prevent you from entering the river.

The second is to leave the road, walk to the left and enter the woods in an effort to give the County building a wide berth and respect the no trespassing restriction. I made the mistake of leaving the river at the riffle upstream of the building (38.358906,-77.637099) with the idea of moving directly north through the woods to intersect the road outside of the trespassing zone. There is no marked trail leading from the river. Instead, there is a dense mass of vegetation woven tight with poison ivy. Once you fight your way through, a high, sheer hill pushes you back towards the river and the thick mass of impenetrable brush. If you choose this route instead of going back to the trail, be sure you have rehearsed the four letter words in your vocabulary because you will use every one of them as the wait-a-minute vines clutch at your legs, poison ivy leaves brush against your face and ticks joyfully drop on your back; happily scurrying towards unmentionable parts of your anatomy.

The third bad choice is try the same tactic of pushing through the brush to wade downstream instead of fighting down the Hunting Run output stream as I will describe in the downstream section. It's a losing proposition given the topography of the high bank and thick brush that protects the County building. The agony of bushwhacking to the right matches the experience to the left.

Hopefully, I convinced you to use Hunting Run Trail. If you do, you will enter the river at exactly the right place to attack the wonderful structure that lies just downriver. At 38.36018,-77.64271, the trail starts to run fairly close to the river and provides the first opportunity to enter the water without a significant amount of bushwhacking. The trail runs out, within 20 feet of the river, at 38.36099,-77.64390 where the river takes a sharp turn to the north.

Unless you are in shape and adventurous, you should focus your fishing activity on the area to the right and fish downstream to the County building. I'll discuss the upstream trek later. If you turn downstream, you find yourself in a broad, open section where the water runs fairly shallow over a bottom that is a mix of jagged rocks with random sandy patches. Even at the height of summer, it does not get overgrown with vegetation; allowing you to catch smallmouth without being constantly hung up. There are two main channels in the river that are obvious from the lighter shade of sand at the bottom.

While initially shallow, walk 25 yards downstream and begin to fish the deep pool underneath a tall bushy tree that marks the upper boundary of a logjam. There is also a small rock ridge that, at low water, points to the base of the tree marking the specific spot. At 38.36006,-77.64158, a line of rocks stretches perpendicular across the river; creating a minor riffle that is mostly visible at low water (50 cfs). Between it and the next line of rocks approximately 40 yards downstream, there is a good, moderately deep channel that deserves careful attention. Fish from the right-hand bank down to the lower boundary at the next line of rocks downstream.

The ideal fishing in this section starts at 38.35971,-77.64102. Even at 50 cfs and below, the channel in the center of the river runs 3 to 4 feet deep. On a clear water day, you can see the fantastic structure hidden underneath the surface of the water. It's full of ragged rocks and ridges with plenty of sheltered pools providing hiding places for bass. In fact, I need to use the word "infested" when describing the quantity of bass you will encounter between here and the other end of the County building. Carefully approach this spot; continuing to fish from the right-hand bank towards the center. As you move downriver, slide left so you can fish underneath the overhanging vegetation that starts approximately 20 yards downstream of the lower line of rocks. The deep section extends all the way from the opposite bank where there is another line of rocks stretching from left to the center. The gap between the end of the rock line and the right-hand bank defines the deep channel.

It remains deep against the right-hand bank all the way down to the logjam at the right edge of the river. If you draw an imaginary line from that point out to a solitary rock that is usually visible and extend it to another logjam in the middle of the river, the line defines a ridge that permits movement to the left-hand bank. It is too deep to wade beyond the ridge, but perfect to fish. Using the ridge line as your platform, fish as far into the deep area as you can. If you are adventurous, you can cling to the vegetation on the right-hand bank and move farther down to fish into the pockets at the bend in the river.

Once on the left-hand bank, fish into the grass beds that mark the turn in the river at 38.35912,-77.63845 as it runs towards the County building. When the water is higher, it's worth fishing the channel that hugs the grass beds and then levels out on a broad shallow shelf at the left-hand side. If the water is low, don't spend much time here because there is better, deeper water downstream below the line of rocks that marks the start of the "lake" in front of the County building. Below the final rapid that leads into the County building stretch, the rocky shelf extends approximately 30 yards downstream. The walking is easiest on the left-hand bank where the sandbars provide a platform to fish into the center of the lake. Fish the right-hand bank, if the water permits, because the rock structure persists on that side all the way down to the base of the County building. Even though there is sand on the left-hand bank, there are large boulders and other rocks hidden in the deep water just beyond the dropoff. Fish deep to catch the largest fish.

Continue downstream on the sandbar to hit the good water on the far side of the County building. The bend in the river at 38.360262,-77.633001 offers another good complex of rocks and grass.

Fishing the "recommended mix" that includes a little of both the up and downstream sections allows you to fish the best of both worlds without signing up for a significant physical challenge.

This is the entrance to the Hunting Run Trail that leads to the optimum start position upstream of the County building.

Downstream from the entry point at a dramatic summer low of 29 cfs.

The structure on the left-hand bank shelters the deeper water.

This logjam is a key landmark leading into the turn to the County building. It is deep on either side and the rock ridge that runs 45° across the river passes in front of it.

This solitary rock is on the right-hand end of the 45° ridge. Sneak up on the spot and fish the deep water beyond; focusing on the structure to the right.

If you stand at the solitary rock and look upriver, the deep section is next to the bank that precedes the rocky ridge.

Smallmouth structure does not get any better than this. Even at the dramatic summer lows we experienced in 2010, it was over 6 feet deep.

This is the "logjam landmark" as seen from downstream. The ridge is your ticket across – don't ignore the deep channels on either side.

At the turn, there are grass beds that precede the deep lake that leads up to the County building in the distance.

At summer lows, the rippled, cracked structure of the ridges push up against a steep hillside supporting a tangle of wait-a-minute vines.

For comparison, this is the view upriver at 71 cfs. Note that much of the rock structure is now underwater. You can still maneuver as long as the water is clear and you can see where you're stepping.

The deep section near the left-hand bank at 71 cfs. At that level, it starts to become marginal in terms of reaching it from downstream.

Finally, at high water in Spring, 314 cfs in this picture, the river is closed out from downstream.

Basically, if kayakers can have fun, you can't wade.

The only way to approach the deep lake in front of the County building is from the opposite shore. Not only is it unsafe, but it is also impassable next to the concrete wall. The banks leading up to the wall are steep with a dramatic drop – no shoreline ledge.

Once you are on the northern bank, use the extensive sandbars and shallow shelf to attack the lake.

Upstream

After enjoying the deep water downstream from the entry point described above, your optimism for the prospects upstream will be unbounded. Be sure and get those emotions under control because I am about to describe a three mile forced march (one way) to get to the best water on the Rapidan outside of the confluence (technically, the confluence is the Rappahannock anyway). To reach it, you have to put up with a long walk across marginal water.

From the entry point upriver for the next half mile, the river runs shallow over a rocky bottom that is mostly flat shelf. There is no clear path for the river in the stretch. As a result of that, the smallmouth could be anywhere they can find cover and their ability to do so will be dependent on the water level. At a gage reading of 50 cfs and below, don't expect to have any action in this area. It gets worse before it gets better. Recognize that, including the walk from your vehicle, you are approximately a mile up the river at this point.

It will be obvious, but at 38.36707, -77.64410, in the middle of the bend, the river becomes totally desolate with a sandy, desert bottom. Late in the day, you may catch a smallmouth "on patrol", but this spot is normally without merit. If you decide to fish rather than skip this part, the better channel is along the left bank. Press on! Your morale will improve another 0.2 miles upriver as you cross a brief, rocky section (38.36901, -77.64272). Farther north, there is a wide expanse of what looks like deep water interspersed with rock ridges and protruding boulders. Sadly, even though the river is scenic with two massive overhanging trees on the left-hand side throwing a significant amount of shade on the water, it remains shallow and sandy for another 0.2 miles.

The next landmark is a group of high sand dunes punctuated by a medium-size tree perched on the high ground in the middle of the river (38.370557,-77.639405). Everything downstream of the tree is shallow and uninteresting, but the area above the dune marks the start of a brief run of good water. You are about a mile and a half from your vehicle. The next 0.2 miles features a return to the rocky bottom;

pockmarked and speckled with vegetation that is attractive to all types of fish. At higher water levels, you can fish horizontally across the river and never be in a bad place. The deeper channel runs on the right. Fish this area hard because it is the last fishable section until you reach 38.37535, -77.63928, another 0.4 miles upstream. Stick with it... it gets better.

After fishing the brief scattering of smallmouth friendly rock structure to include the deep channel where the river drops across a small set of rapids just upstream at 38.37632, -77.63988, "man up" and walk another 0.2 miles to finally reach the start of the "promised land". En route you get to fish a deep pool below a small waterfall that forms the lower boundary of a "confluence-like" stretch. Follow the current of the river around to the right and stay with it to climb the dramatic drop in elevation that deposits you at the tail of a 50 yard lake. The deep channel runs along the right bank and you have to cross early. The best place is just downstream from a private picnic area (38.378177,-77.648208) created by the landowner on the right-hand bank.

Stay in the channel of the river and fish until you draw even with the picnic bench that sits on a high ridge overlooking the lake. Walk out on the shelf that can be waist deep or more and cast as far as you are able into the 10 to 15 deep water that extends across the river to the southern shore. Slowly scoot around the perimeter of this deep area; fishing as you go. In the heat of the summer, the smallmouth concentrate in this location to take advantage of the deep pockets where the water remains cool. There are a few large boulders lurking just beneath the surface of the water; target those. The upper boundary of the lake is marked with a short uphill climb as the river spills down another gentle gradient break. Follow the main current of the river as it winds around. There are a limited number of deeper holes carved into the floor of the river and the best way to find them is to let the river show you as it changes color; deeper shades of green indicate deeper water.

While I could continue to walk you up the river since I have actually waded all the way between Hunting Run and Elys Ford, I'll cut off this description at the place that marks the midpoint and pick up the discussion in the next chapter. Above the small gradient break, at 38.37614, -77.65204 , where the river takes a sharp turn to the right, is another medium-size lake. Depending on the water level, this may be the end of your walk upstream unless you exit the river and fight your way through the brush on the bank. If you can wade, stick to the center and cast towards either bank. Although there is a minimal amount of structure clustered along the edges, the shade provides a compelling attraction to the smallmouth during the heat of the day. I stood in one spot and caught five fish in a row throwing to a small pocket of shade on the southern bank. It is equally productive on the northern bank. Unless you are going to hike all the way through to Elys Ford, this is the midpoint and you are 3.53 miles, as the angler wanders, from your vehicle. If you have the physical capability to get to this last mile upriver -- either walking or using a kayak or canoe -- it is well worth the effort.

At 37 cfs, the river is at decent levels and features optimum wading as you move upstream from the entry point.

After the initial good rocky structure, the river becomes broad and featureless as it transitions into a sandy bottom.

The brown sheen glimmering up through the slack water leads to a sandbar on the right and confirms poor smallmouth bass habitat. Skip through.

After the desert, you enter a brief section that is fishable.

The solitary tree on top of the sandbar is at the upper left of this picture.

Immediately upstream from the tree, the river becomes fishable again with the bottom transitioning to a mix of sand and rock.

Continuing around the bend, fish your way to the next "dead zone."

Hang your rod on your shoulder and hike through this unproductive section.

Finally! The waterfall at the head of the grassy islands denotes the start of a minor "confluence" type environment.

The picnic table is on the bank to the right of this picture. Carefully fish the deep section to the left using the ledge that reaches from the right-hand bank.

The area above the lake is fishable as well. You can wade anywhere in the river in this spot.

This is the riffle break that marks the downstream boundary of one of the best "lakes" in this section. It is the lower boundary of some of the best fishing on the Rapidan.

Immediately upstream from the lake, the river runs around the bend to the left and enters the confluence-like area. But don't skip the lake. The bass huddle underneath the trees at the left.

There's a deep channel that runs next to the bank. You may have problems depending on the water level. At 44 cfs, the water will be up to your chest.

The goal! This is the view looking upstream into the smallmouth infested section of the Rapidan at the big bend in the river.

In particular, the deep section immediately on the other side of the grass bed holds spectacular smallies. The bank is deepest to the left.

Downstream

Get prepared for a tough physical challenge. If you read the upstream section regarding how to reach the river when you encounter the "no trespassing" sign, your immediate question should be, "Why can't I dodge through the woods, heading downstream, to avoid the off-limits area?" The answer lies in the nature of the woods to the right of the sign. It's hilly, thick and requires more exertion to make it to the river than going the way I am about to describe.

If you don't want to follow Hunting Run Trail and, assuming you follow my advice and don't try and cut through the woods, your only other option is to walk from the parking area down the overgrown dirt road towards the output stream from Hunting Run Reservoir. The stream is your highway to the river.

Be careful as you approach the output stream since the brush is thick on either side of an opening guarded by a collection of loose boulders. Exercise due caution and carefully climb down the boulder pile to reach the streambed. If you are a true fishing addict, have your rod rigged up because there are a few pools between the dam and the river. Granted, these are mostly small sunfish, but I saw a 12 inch smallie trapped in one. The vegetation on either side of the stream is tight and forces you to the center of the stream until you come to a large beaver dam at 38.35574, -77.63522. The beaver dam captured all the silt that swept out of Hunting Run Reservoir. As such, both banks are mostly mud and you will sink up to your thighs if you try and walk down the middle. Cling to the brush on either side so if you step into a deep pocket, you can pull yourself out.

Downstream of the beaver dam, the stream begins to look like trout water; full of rocks and ridges with cuts that run a foot or two deep through chiseled channels. Eventually, the stream bottoms out in the valley a short distance from the Rapidan. You know you are close to your goal when the vegetation opens up and the water becomes stagnant as a result of the lack of heavy flow from the reservoir. Walking becomes easy at this point. Although you'll be happy to finally see it, don't run up to the junction with the Rapidan (38.35936, -77.63409). There is a deep pool at the confluence that needs to be fished. It is a mile hike to reach this point from the parking area. Hopefully, just the description of the challenge to follow this path to the river will convince you to take the extra time and enjoy the good fishing downstream of the Hunting Run Trail access point!

To fish downstream, move along the shoreline until the water shallows out near the bend (38.359684,-77.634097) where the river charges north. This is an unusually good spot that merits a decent amount of time. Unless floods have washed them downstream, there are a few fallen logs in the middle of the river hung up on the rocks that are scattered across the bend. Wherever you can find a logjam, fish it carefully since the big boys hang out nearby. The bend is full of channels where the river carved multiple paths through the rocky bottom. Fish the channels, but do not ignore the southern bank. The amount of overhanging vegetation provides a shady refuge. If you splash along the bank, you'll be startled and disappointed to see an amazing number of big fish dart from the shoreline. Use caution and float blue or green poppers along any vegetation under the shade.

This continues until you reach 38.361263,-77.632572 where the river takes a slight bend to the right at a line of rocks. At this position, the river transitions to a sandy bottom with the good rock structure on the right-hand side. There are fish in this section and it represents the last good "shallow" water until you reach the confluence. However, if the weather has been hot and the water levels are low, the smallmouth will migrate to the deep spots to hunker near the bottom where the water is coolest.

In this section, the deep spot is along the eastern bank at 38.364561,-77.630535. In fact, the river becomes so deep, you will have a hard time wading farther downriver when the water is above 40 cfs unless you hug the western bank. Even then, you may be forced out of the water and have to bushwhack along the shore to reach the next good rocky section that starts at 38.365587,-77.630259. When you get to the deep channel, put on a lot of weight and run your lure next the bottom.

This is where you have the highest probability of catching a trophy fish at the height of summer.

Welcome to the streambed below the Hunting Run Reservoir!

There is some tough bushwhacking.

Once you reach the river, this is the view downstream from the junction at 314 cfs.

If you turn to the left, this is the view upstream. At 314 cfs, you have to pick your way carefully and will probably be closed out before you get too far. This section of the river is best fished at lower water levels.

The rocks reemerge closer to the downstream bank and, at 40 cfs, reveal dramatic formations of rocks framed by numerous grass beds.

The rocks continue into the ridge structure upstream.

Bottom Line

If you have a lot of energy and are in good physical condition, you may want to do the 3.5 mile hike upstream at least once. Otherwise, you can spend a good day within a half mile, upstream and down, of the County building that marks the center. The water is deep, full of rocks and boulders, and holds a great population of smallmouth and sunfish.

Elys Ford

Google Map Coordinates: 38.359157,-77.685742

Summary Rating

Parking	**Green**	Spin Fishing	**Green**
Canoe/Kayak Launch	**Green**	Fly Fishing	**Green**
Distance to River	**Green**	Trout	**Red**
Can Bike to River	**Red**	Smallmouth Bass	**Green**
Physical Fitness	**Green**	Pressure	**Yellow**
Scenery	**Yellow**	Overall	**Green**

The opportunities a short distance upstream at the bend in the river, combined with the superb structure 3.5 miles downstream, drive the overall rating to green. If you are only willing to wade a mile from the parking lot, go upstream. The mile immediately downstream from the access point is not worth the energy.

Special Regulations

There are no special fishing regulations in effect at this location.

Getting to the Stream

From I-95, take exit 130B onto VA 3 W (Plank Rd) toward Culpeper. Turn right on VA 610 (Elys Ford Road). Follow it to the bridge over the Rapidan. The parking area is on the southeast side of the bridge (38.359157,-77.685742).

Canoe/Kayak Comment: Elys Ford is one of only two formal VDGIF maintained launch sites on the Rapidan. As such, this is a popular place in the summer and the large parking area fills up. If you launch here, you could take out at Hunting Run if you are willing to portage your boat 0.7 miles up the hill to the parking area by following the Hunting Run Trail. Otherwise, the Clore Brothers launch is the next take-out downriver.

Environment and Fish

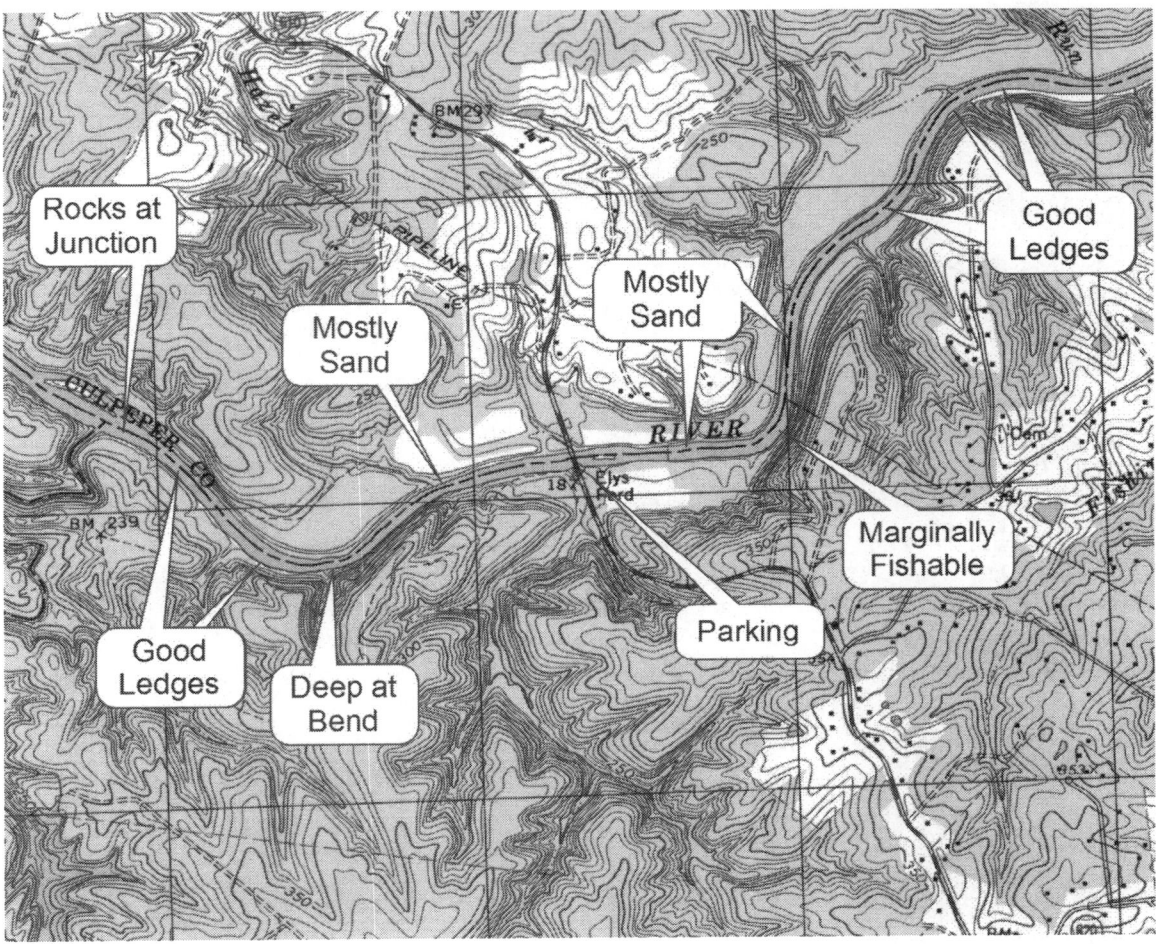

If you fished the Confluence before wandering out to Elys Ford and expect the rest of the river to match the spectacular nature of the fishing there, you are doomed to being disappointed. The closest match to the confluence is the Harpers Ferry to Brunswick section of the Upper Potomac that I discuss in my book, *Wade and Shoreline Fishing the Potomac River for Smallmouth Bass*.

Anyway, the general topography of Elys is that of a flat, gently flowing river. Your fishing experience upstream will be markedly different than if you go down unless you are willing to wade several miles. In terms of access, the city property stretches downstream from the parking lot to the east. Other than that, all other parts of the shoreline are private property. Therefore, if you head upstream, you must stay in the river to avoid trespassing. Downstream, you can exit the river on the southern side and usually be on public land.

Upstream

Your first challenge, if you decide to go upstream, is to determine where to enter the river. You may be tempted to cross the road and walk upstream on the shoreline to put some distance between you and the parking area. Not only would that violate private property, but if you walk over to the west edge of the road and peer intently into the woods, it presents an impenetrable barrier of thick scrub brush, clinging vines and poison ivy. Therefore, you need to resolve yourself to slogging up the river.

Enter the water cautiously from the parking lot and make an instant, personal assessment of whether it's going to be too deep and too fast for you to negotiate. In general, the center of the river is where it is the shallowest. There are many deep sections in the vicinity of the bridge and you have to feel your way around. Once beyond the bridge, you may as well start fishing right away since the next 800 yards are all the same.

The river bottom between the bridge and the bend is uniformly sandy and barren. There are deeper sections on either shoreline sheltered by overhanging vegetation or fallen logs. These are the only places that will hold fish. There are some smallmouth here, but mostly you will hit sunfish as you move up to the bend in the river. Many of the sunfish are huge and will give you a jolt if you are fishing on light tackle. If you are a smallmouth fanatic, and that is the only species you are after, you could become discouraged and consider turning back. Don't do that, the walk to the bend is worth it.

At the bend (38.356318,-77.695345), the rocks begin. The first target is the bend itself. There is a rocky shelf that extends perpendicular for most of the distance across the river that allows you to move to the middle and fish the deep cut that guides the main current flow. The farther you can get your lure down low in the channel, the more likely it is that you will catch a larger fish. You can attack from the perpendicular ridge line or from downstream by wading as close as you can get using the sandy peninsula that stretches towards the middle of the downstream part of the bend. Spin anglers will have a definite advantage given that the pace of the current picks up as the river careens around the corner. Fly rodders will have a hard time pushing a streamer close to the bottom – even with a sinking line. Besides, it is not worth the hassle of putting one on just for this single spot. With spin gear, you can load up on weight and get a plastic worm or grub down next to the bottom where it will attract the attention of the big guys.

After fishing the bend, look upstream and be happy. The tops of innumerable boulders rise up through the surface of the river to build the perpendicular ridge structures that form the basis of the river bottom for the next 800 yards.

While you should not skip over anything, the next good location is approximately 100 yards up from the bend. There is a complex of submerged logs that are hung up in a deep pool that you cannot wade across. Hopefully, the logs are still there and not been pushed downstream by flooding. Move to the left side of the river using the extended rock shelf to avoid the deep water and spooking the fish. I've stood here in the past and thrown small poppers above the log structure and caught fish on every cast. Start the approach at least 10 feet above the structure and float the popper downstream; twitching when you get over the logs. Use heavier tippet to put instant pressure on the fish to keep them close to the surface and avoid wrapping the line around the branches below.

Once you've played out this spot, continue upstream to the junction of Wilderness Run (38.360369,-77.70308) that joins the river from the south. Between the "log hole" and Wilderness Run, the good rock structure thins out. While there are still plenty of parallel ridges, they are separated by sandy sections. If you fish the sand, concentrate on the right-hand side of the river where it is a little deeper and shade hangs over the river. Be sure and look for the minor ridge complex at 38.358699,-77.699293 (300 yards upstream from the bend) and the more prominent rocky composition another 75 yards upstream at 38.359494,-77.70013.

Once you reach the mouth of Wilderness Run, it's only worth going another hundred yards upstream before you reach a sandy desert. At that point, you are 1.1 miles from your vehicle.

Looking downstream to the bridge from midway to the first bend in the river. There is no structure here – mostly sand. The fish hug the banks.

The view upstream into the good corner. Fish quickly between the bridge and the corner. The good fishing starts there.

After the corner, there is a good section of rock ridges. The deep water is towards the right-hand bank.

Looking back towards the corner from across the first "lake" upstream. Look for a cluster of sunken logs on the right-hand side.

Near Wilderness Run at 38 cfs. Fish the rocks and return to your truck.

The view downstream from the turnaround point.

Downstream

It is amazing how different your experience can be if you decide to go downstream versus up. Until you fish all of the access points, you should fish in both directions and not be prejudiced by me. That said, my perspective is that, at this location, downstream is a bad experience unless you're willing to walk a "significant" distance. Since the definition of "significant" depends on your personal level of physical fitness, I will describe the downstream trek all the way to the superb water 3.43 miles from the launch. Make your own call on where to turn around, but, upfront, unless you are willing to wade for more than a mile, don't even think about going downstream since it will be a waste of time. If you decide to wade all the way to the good area, be sure you have the strength to wade back against the strong push of the current.

After parking in the lot to the east of the bridge, walk down the canoe ramp to enter the river. Do not ignore fishing underneath the bridge and on the right-hand bank as it goes around the island formed beneath the metal bridge piling. The more I fish, the more I discover that many of the easy access points are lightly pressured because everyone assumes the opposite. If this changes, you'll discover it quickly enough. Do not make the mistake of dawdling in the bad water if you are going to target the exceptional water that lies in the downstream distance.

While recent flooding cleared off the sand that coated the river bottom for the first 600 yards, it's still tragically shallow once you get downstream of the island (38.359477,-77.684519) near the bridge. In fact, instead of walking in the streambed and burning energy pushing water, you should follow the small trail that leads eastward from the parking lot through the city property bordering the river on the southern bank. It gives you a high perch above the river and allows you to make your own judgment about when and where to enter the river.

I prefer to walk on the trail all the way to the bend and begin fishing at the rocky ridge that stretches entirely across the river (38.35999,-77.679192). At that point, there are numerous serrated rock ridges that run at a 45° angle into the bend from upstream. They create channels that need to be fished individually. The biggest pool is at the bend itself. For the next 300 yards, the river deepens in the middle and has marginal rock structure on the eastern shoreline. Once you reach the bend, move to the right-hand bank to target the channel hugging the left-hand bank. There's a shallow shelf that runs up the left-hand bank making fishing directly underneath the trees unproductive. Walk out on the serrated rock ridges to work the deep channel in the middle of the river.

"Deep channel" is a relative term. It's certainly deeper on the left-hand side than it is on the right, but not deep enough to hold any water interesting to large fish. As you fish through 38.36206,-77.67816, your opportunity to catch smallmouth is limited unless the water is high. At summer lows, you should skip this and look for the next deep water downstream.

Move to the left and fish towards the right-hand side where the remnants of the rock ridges remain. There are some deep channels that may hold fish, but at summer water levels, you may as well skip them and move farther downstream. The closer you get to the next bend in the river, the more the bottom transitions to sand without a rock in sight. You should turn around at 38.36333,-77.678211 (0.75 miles from the parking lot) or commit yourself to an extremely long walk to the next good structure that is another 0.4 miles farther downstream (38.369454,-77.672739). Sadly, this is where wading has its limitations. Kayakers or canoeists can selectively fish downstream to overnight at the Confluence, enjoy the great fishing there, and then proceed to the take-out at Motts Run the following day.

Continue downstream until you see the rock formation that stretches out to match the tip of a radically leaning tree. Fish both sides of the rock formation. Do not ignore the area immediately behind it since there is another large hole between the rock and the base of the tree. Beyond the rock, continue to fish on the left from the high ridge created by the sand in the center of the river. The right-hand bank, although populated with blowdowns, is shallow and uninteresting. Be sure to pay attention to the small grass island approximately 35 yards upstream of the rock. The river carved a five foot deep pool in front of the rock and it holds smallies even at low water in the summer. The grass bed marks the point that is approximately 1.1 miles from the parking area.

Don't forget to fish the deep channel on either side of the bridge.

This is the downstream channel immediately adjacent to the parking lot at 37 cfs.

The corner at 37 cfs. Shallow and unproductive.

The corner at 203 cfs holds fish.

Around the corner, the deep channel on the left holds fish at higher water levels,.

At summer lows, you get a good look at the serrated rock ridge that stretches downstream from the bend.

For a mile downstream, most of the water is wide, sandy and barren. In the ebook, these pictures are in color and the brown sheen of the sand glares through.

The rocks at the top of this picture are the turnaround point if you only want to wade for a mile.

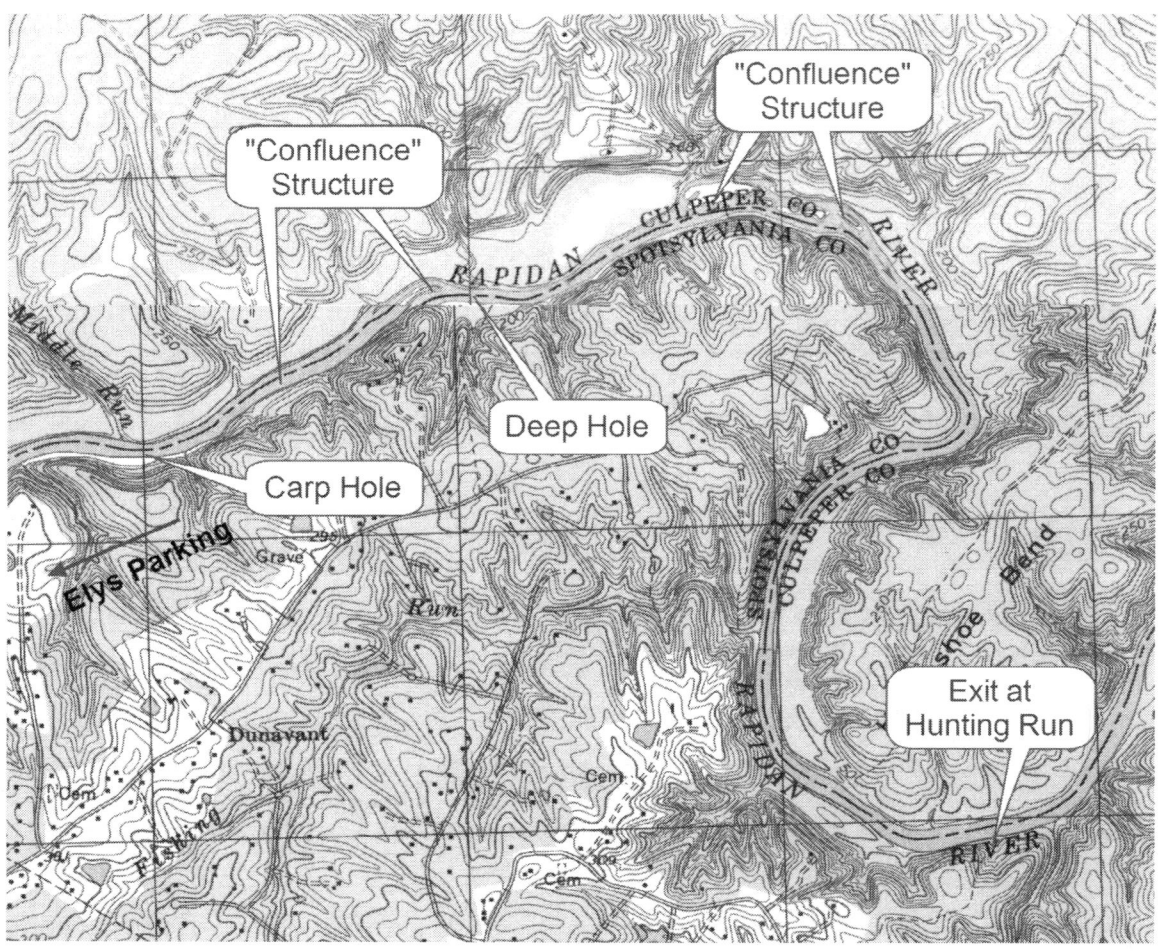

The river deepens upstream of the grass island, with the channel clinging to the left bank. The bottom is sandy, so walk through quickly; only targeting the rocky areas. At summer lows, you will not have any problem wading up the center of the river, but when the water is higher, stick to the right-hand bank. The bottom is sandy and unproductive until reaching the rock garden. At higher water levels, the log complex at 38.36558,-77.67688 is worth a few throws. When the water is low, skip it and move upriver. Don't get overly excited at the prospect of the rocks in front of you. They are surrounded by a flat, sandy uninteresting bottom. If there are smallmouth, they will hang on the right-hand side where numerous rock ridges cut through the shallow water and create channels that hold sunfish.

At summer lows, this entire area is very shallow. 38.36724,-77.67445 marks the center of a rock complex where the river turns to the northwest at a slight bend. The ridges run parallel with the direction of flow; creating channels that can be up to 2 feet deep. The left edge of the river remains a solid desert of featureless sand while the right bank has interesting structure. If you cast perpendicular to the flow of the river, use a weedless presentation or face constant hang ups. A good approach in this section is to use poppers or other top water lures that can dance across the ridge lines and attract the fish sitting a foot or two below.

The river stays sandy through the start of the turn leading into the next corner 38.370195,-77.672144. After working the cliff face at 38.36955,-77.67267, continue to hug the right river bank. The left bank is mostly shallow while the right bank is marginally wadeable. If you pick your path carefully, you can walk along the sand ridge between the deep channel to the left and the bank to the right. Fish up against the bank , under the overhanging trees and next to the structure on the right. All of the logjams piled up on the right-hand bank hold fish; even at low water levels in the middle of the summer.

At 38.37058,-77.67067, the river returns to being shallow as it leads into the second significant complex of rocks. They run at the standard 45° across the river and are surrounded by a thick coat of sand. This makes the center of the river unattractive to fish, but the right bank continues to be productive. Starting at 38.36955,-77.67267, be prepared to see schools of carp, to include massive 3 to 4 foot long monsters. Smallmouth follow them to eat the leftovers kicked up as the carp nose along the bottom. Skip through the second rock garden, it's all shallow. Move down to 38.37052,-77.66784 where there is a large, tangled blowdown stretched along the right-hand shore. It is deep on that side and, in addition to the carp, you can pick up some smallmouth up against the edges of the structure. 38.37045,-77.66759 (where Middle Run empties into the Rapidan from the north) is the deepest hole so far on the Rapidan. Fish up against the blowdown that stretches 30° into the river from the right bank. It stays deep downstream for approximately 30 yards. Work it from the center.

Just downstream of the log, there is a ledge perpendicular to the shore that provides an attractive holding area for both catfish and smallmouth. Once you fish the upstream side of the ledge, you can use it to walk to the shore and throw against the submerged logs that line the base of the bank. The deep water on either side needs attention. If the water level is high, you will be unable to fish the additional ledge that is just downriver. In fact, as you move downriver, the depth forces you to the left bank where it remains sandy; putting most anglers out of casting range of the good spot.

When the water is high, this will be the end of your wading downstream unless you get out on the left-hand bank and dodge around the deep pool that collects at the downstream end of carp heaven. At 38.37115,-77.66506, the river makes a slight jog to the left to run down a small set of rapids. This is where the river begins to look exactly like the confluence. Stretched in front of you is a fascinating array of short pools; each with its own perimeter marked by rock ridges running across the river. The river bottom is perfect smallmouth habitat; full of rocks and ridges with enough vegetation to produce the appropriate amount of food. Depending on the time of the year, many of the pools will be too shallow to hold anything significant. If you are here late in the year, move downstream and pick your spots based on the depth of the run. Stay to the left and follow the main current. The right bank gets shallow.

In the vicinity of 38.37360,-77.66040, the river takes a run to the right and then S-curves to the left. Small smallmouth skitter out of your way; running in every direction. *This area is infested with bass.* If you fish the deep pools, you will be able to catch as many 8 to 12 inch bass as you care to pull in. Just stay with the main current and you will find the fish. At 38.37498,-77.65814, the river turns sharply to the south and reveals the largest "lake" in the mini-confluence. Stay as far to the left as you can while remaining within casting distance of the right-hand channel; that is where the fish are.

In fact, the big lake is really deep on the right-hand bank just downstream of the headwater with the last half of the pool being shallow featuring large rocks coated with tufts of grass. The drop-off in depth near the right-hand bank is abrupt with plenty of fish cooling themselves in the shade. At this point, you stand 3.43 miles from the entry point and, and unless you plan to walk all the way down to the Hunting Run access point, you should turn around here. To get to Hunting Run, it's another 3.53 miles of tough walking in the river with no side trails along the shore to make your life easy when you hit bad water. But, on the plus side, the water pushes in that direction; making it an easier choice than going back to Elys Ford.

You start to see additional structure on either bank. This should key you to the right-hand side where there is a deep stretch leading up to a rock ridge that pokes out from the right-hand side.

At the rock ridge, take the time to fish this spot carefully. It is deep up against the logs at the right-hand side of the picture. Fish here and around the corner. Skip the next section.

At summer lows of 40 cfs or below, the rock garden is unproductive.

Continue downriver into you reach this spot – it is particularly deep and supports a vibrant population of massive carp and smallmouth.

This is the start of the "mini-confluence." Be careful where you step because fingerling size smallmouth bass skitter in every direction.

Each ridge creates a pool that holds bass. In fact, this section of the river is infested with fish. Every channel holds something interesting and each rock shelters a pool.

The grass islands provide an interesting patchwork of channels.

This is the final "lake" that marks 3.43 miles of walking from the Elys Ford parking area. You can continue down to Hunting Run if you are willing to stay in the river for another 3.53 miles. See the Hunting Run chapter for the description.

Bottom Line

Elys Ford is a ok place to spend the day. Depending on your physical capability and your energy level, you have several good opportunities. The quick trip to the better water is to fish upstream all the way to Wilderness Run. If you are a hard-core, addicted and physically capable angler, gear up for a 7+ mile round trip of tough wading and head downstream. Unless you are willing to walk more than a mile, downstream is a poor choice.

Germanna (Route 3 Bridge)

Google Map Coordinates: 38.379143,-77.785006

Summary Rating

Parking	Red	Spin Fishing	Green
Canoe/Kayak Launch	Yellow	Fly Fishing	Green
Distance to River	Yellow	Trout	Red
Can Bike to River	Red	Smallmouth Bass	Green
Physical Fitness	Yellow	Pressure	Yellow
Scenery	Green	Overall	Green

The overall Green rating applies more to the upstream stretch than downstream.

Special Regulations

There are no special fishing regulations in effect at this location.

Getting to the Stream

From I-95, take exit 130B onto VA 3 W (Plank Rd) toward Culpeper. Follow it to the bridge over the Rapidan that is just beyond the Memorial Foundation of the Germanna Colonies in Virginia. Do not park on the grounds of the foundation since they have an aggressive towing program.

If you would like to park on the grounds, others have told me that you can buy a pass to access the river for $100. Given the VDOT easement, it's not worth it.

You only have two options to park at the bridge and both are on the east side. The entire west side of the bridge is too tight with a steel guardrail limiting any opportunity to pull off safely. The road leading up to the east side of the bridge offers wide shoulders that allow you to tuck your vehicle a significant distance away from the main road. That said, there is clearly a winner between the east and westbound choices dictated by the easier accessibility to the river below. The eastbound side at 38.378874,-77.784534 provides both room and admission. As with any of these VDOT based access points, you must pay attention to evolving traffic regulations that may put this off-limits in the future. As of the date this book went to the publisher, there is no signage restricting parking.

It is a steep climb over some large rocks to get down to the sandy river bottom under the bridge. If you follow the beaten path, it will take you down a slick, muddy hill that is actually harder to negotiate than climbing carefully over the boulder field under the bridge. As with everywhere in Virginia, there is plenty of poison ivy, so be prepared to wash off with poison ivy soap after you fish.

Canoe/Kayak Comment: If you don't mind bumping your boat across a rock or sliding it down a mud slicked hill as you dodge through the underbrush, it is possible to launch a boat.

Environment and Fish

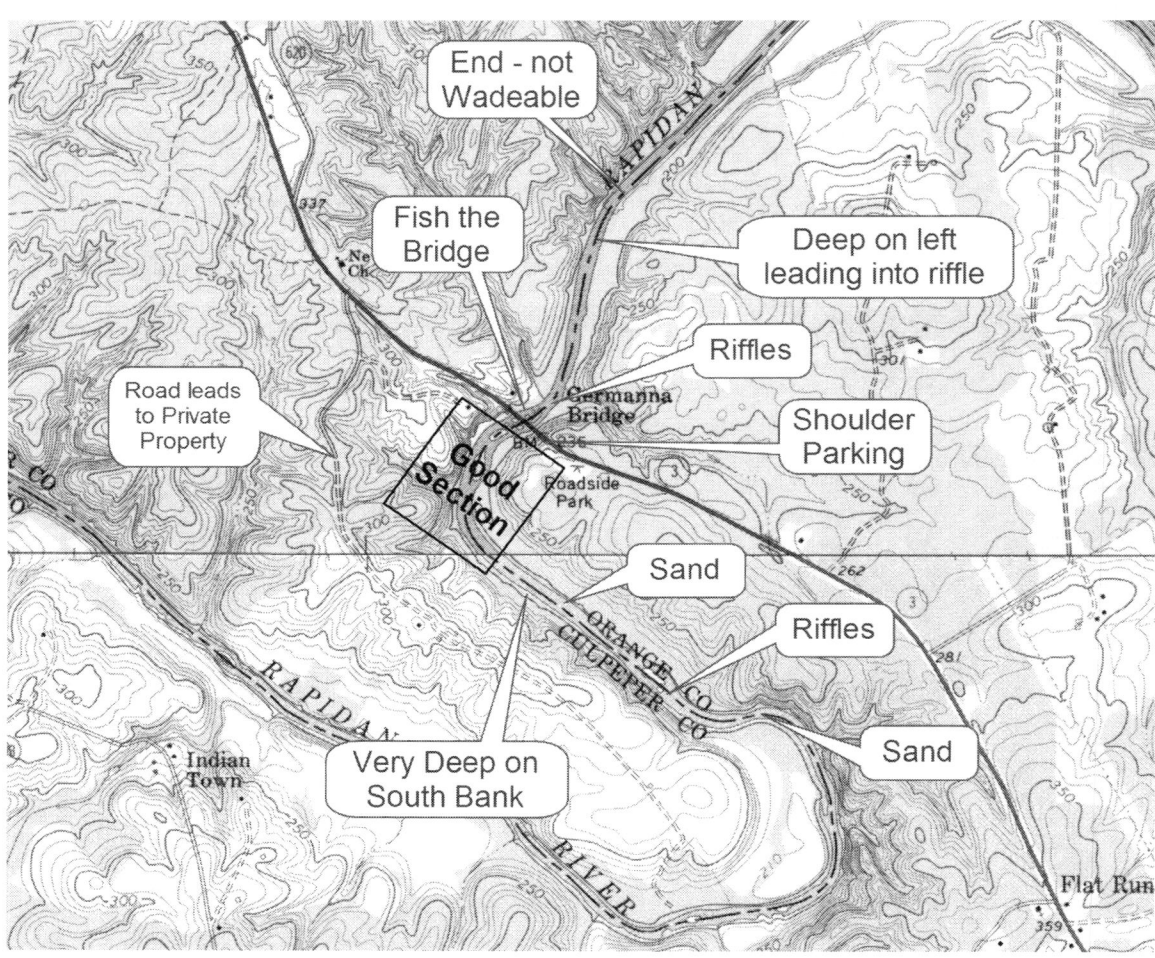

The Germanna access point exemplifies the good fishing that is available in the lower section of the river. Upstream provides the better choice, but downstream is almost as good. The river is broken into frequent islands surrounded by plenty of rock structure with elevation drops that allow fast-moving water to push the sand and silt downstream.

Upstream

It's a tough choice to decide which way to go when you stand underneath the bridge. In my mind, there is no contest. Head upstream. The first third of a mile offers superb fishing framed by islands, grassy clumps and boulder structure that all holds good fish in moderately deep, yet wadeable water. At the end of that third of a mile, you face a long, deep sandy stretch before you reach the next interesting water 800 yards in the distance.

For those of you who believe you have to separate yourself from the access point before you reach good fishing, don't make the mistake and ignore the section immediately under the bridge. Begin to fish your way up the numerous cuts and runs that provide paths through the complex island structure. While you won't catch any monsters in the shallow water, you get a good warm-up with 8 to 12 inch bass that seem to like the protection and food this area offers. It won't be apparent at river level, but there are two main channels, separated by a two large islands, that feed into the bridge. The channel on the left is the narrower of the two. Therefore, you should fish it first since you will spook the fish if you hit it moving downstream. The channel runs about for 300 yards on the left-hand side of two large islands. At lower water, you will need to abandon this channel. If the water looks bad at the base, don't bother to fish it.

As you move up the left-hand channel, pay special attention to the break between the two islands that occurs at 38.378372,-77.786921. If the water is low, this is a good place to switch sides. But don't flip and fish upstream from here. Instead, go back to the bridge and work up the channel that hugs the right-hand bank of the river. The first thing you encounter after fishing through the narrower runs is a large pool, about 15 yards wide, 35 yards long and 2 feet deep, which has thick, overhanging vegetation on the shoreline. In fact, the best area to fish is close to the shoreline with pools approaching 4 or 5 feet deep. You should fish this area from the island to the shore to avoid spooking the fish and hit all of the deeper sections. Wade upstream, working back and forth until you reach a small grassy clump/island offset from the tip of the main island at 38.378439,-77.787221. Fish both sides of the clump and make a decision – continue or quit?

The river widens as it turns to the southeast and gets very deep. In fact, I recommend you only attack this section in the summer when you can wet wade because you will certainly step in the wrong place and fill up your waders - something to avoid when the water is cold. You should wear a PFD regardless of the season. There is decent access along the left bank, but you cannot travel on the right-hand side as a result of its great depth. The right-hand bank tortures you with good structure - fallen trees, overhanging trees, logs askew - that you cannot reach because it is too deep to wade within casting range. These all provide perfect shelter for the big fish. If you use spin gear, you have a better shot since you can add additional weight to provide the leverage needed for a long throw.

About 400 yards into the hike from the bend at 38.376048,-77.787774, there's another shallow section that provides an intermediate objective prior to reaching the better water that occurs at the far turn in the distance. To move upriver, there is more deep water to deal with; so hug the left-hand bank to get through. At the end of the long ramble, there's another good section of rock ledges and boulders at 38.371481,-77.780762. Fish that spot and upstream approximately 50 yards and turn back. Beyond that point, the river takes another jog to the left, deepens and switches to sand. It is not worth continuing based on the quality of fishing in front of you.

Fish the small channels directly upstream from the bridge.

The channels eventually lead into a lake like area that hugs the right-hand bank. Be sure and spend time working the deep water underneath the tree cover on the right-hand bank.

At the top of the lake, beyond the line of rocks, there's a single grass island that has good fishing on either side.

Beyond that point, the river widens and becomes excruciatingly deep on the right-hand side – even at 23 cfs (this picture). You can wade upstream on the left, but it is sandy and unproductive. To be successful, you have to find a way to get your lure into the deep water on the right-hand side.

This is the view upstream at the rock complex where you should turn around.

View downstream from the same point shows that there is minimal rock structure between the grass island and this spot.

Downstream

The standard advice applies here -- fish the bridge. There's a deep spot near the pilings that is shady and usually holds fish. Move downstream, wading over the shallow rocky bottom and ignore the grass bed on the left since it borders a very shallow section of the river. Instead, turn your attention to the right-hand bank and the shady areas underneath the trees. At the end of the grass bed, there is a deep hole. Granted, the river changes character from being a rocky, gravel/cobble bottom to sand, but the depth attracts fish and you need to give it a shot. Once past, turn your interest to the area underneath a large dead tree that looks like a huge spider web on the right-hand side. There's a good, deep cut that runs on the bank all the way up to the gradient break.

Looking downstream, there are some boulders to your left front. Fish around those and then switch to the grass bed on the right that leads into the first riffle stretching across the river at 38.38051,-77.784075. Approximately 150 feet downstream, there is another perpendicular structure. Between those two lines of rocks, the river has a rocky bottom with good sized boulders randomly distributed. Each marks the start of a deeper hole. You can wade down either side of the river; casting to the center since that's where the deeper water is. Don't bother to fish the shoreline beyond the first line of rocks -- it's uniformly shallow and unproductive. Once past the second ridge at 38.381843,-77.783707, move to the right-hand side of the river and try and hold to the center as much as you can. The deeper and better section of the river for the next several hundred yards is on the left. Be sure to use lures that will bump along the bottom, but don't overlook floating small poppers underneath the trees and against the logs.

The next landmark is a large fallen log next to several tall, overhanging trees on the left bank. At that point, the river becomes deep and rocky with emerging ridges. Although it remains sandy on the right-hand side, there are rocks and other subsurface structure on the left that holds fish. It gets shallow in the middle of the summer, but ,when the water is higher, it's worth fishing this section from the fallen log all the way up to the twin rocks that emerge in the distance at the bend in the river (38.38527,-77.78262).

The river is strikingly deep and sandy in the 25 yard stretch leading up to the twin rocks, so approach carefully and work the deep area hard with lures that will stay close to the bottom. After you fish the twin rocks, you may as well move quickly to the next gradient break on the other side of the bend at 38.38663,-77.78107. En route, the river is deeper on the left-hand side and you have the opportunity to float some poppers underneath the overhanging branches, but all you will catch is sunfish.

At the bend, a grass island splits the river into a fast section on the right and slower on the left. There is a deep pool immediately downstream of the island, with plenty of fish waiting for food to sweep through the highly oxygenated water of the break. At normal water levels, this will be the end of your trip since the deep section stretches from bank to bank. Anyway, since you are three quarters of a mile from the bridge, this is a good place to turn around.

It's worth taking a few casts in the deep water near the bridge pilings.

Fish downstream and cover the deep spot to the left of the grass island as well as the channel leading into the "spider web tree" on the right.

Focus your attention on the parts of the river that offer structure. At 314 cfs, the downstream section is easy to wade.

Most of the downstream stretch is open, flat and sandy.

This spot marks your turnaround point. There is a deep lake beyond the rock.

This logjam marks the limit of your downstream wading at higher water levels.

Bottom Line

This is one of the good areas on the Rapidan to fish. The perfect day would be to hit the upstream section and then walk downstream through the first set of good structure. I do not recommend you walk father than the first bend going upstream or the second riffle break going down. Beyond those two locations, the fish are spread out and the bottom switches to sand.

Raccoon Ford

Google Map Coordinates: 38.356215,-77.95493

Summary Rating

Parking	Green	Spin Fishing	Green
Canoe/Kayak Launch	Yellow	Fly Fishing	Green
Distance to River	Yellow	Trout	Red
Can Bike to River	Red	Smallmouth Bass	Green
Physical Fitness	Green	Pressure	Green
Scenery	Yellow	Overall	Red

The flat sandy river bottom and associated lack of compelling smallmouth structure add up to a Red overall rating for this location.

Special Regulations

There are no special fishing regulations in effect at this location.

Getting to the Stream

From US 29 near Culpeper, take US 522 / VA 3 exit towards Culpeper. Turn left onto 15. Turn right onto 522. (in other words, take 29 to 522 and stay on it). From 522, turn left onto Raccoon Ford Rd (VA 611). Follow Raccoon Ford Road for approximately 1.5 miles and look for the small opening in the dense woods on the river side that leads to the parking area (38.356215,-77.95493).

You really have to be careful to find the small VDGIF turnout. The first time you drive by (and you will miss the turn) you will assume that the small dirt road that is the entrance to the parking area is somebody's driveway. It's not marked from the road, so drive slowly until you find it. Basically, if you are on Raccoon Ford heading west, be alert once you come around the bend. If you pass a driveway on the left, you just missed the turnoff into the access point. While you don't need a GPS to find any of the other access points, this is the one where that tool comes in handy.

If you do a thorough map reconnaissance, you may conclude that you can reach the stretch of the river from the north via VA 617. Don't bother. There's no access from that side of the river that does not involve crossing private property. Besides, if you follow that road to the end, and walked across the private property, you would end up at the deep, backed up section behind the old dam. Not wadeable.

Canoe/Kayak comment: This is a well developed and established put-in point. The parking area is right next to the river. You have to slide your kayak or canoe down a steep, very narrow trail to reach the rivers edge. There is no beach or ledge at river. The hill ends at the water.

Environment and Fish

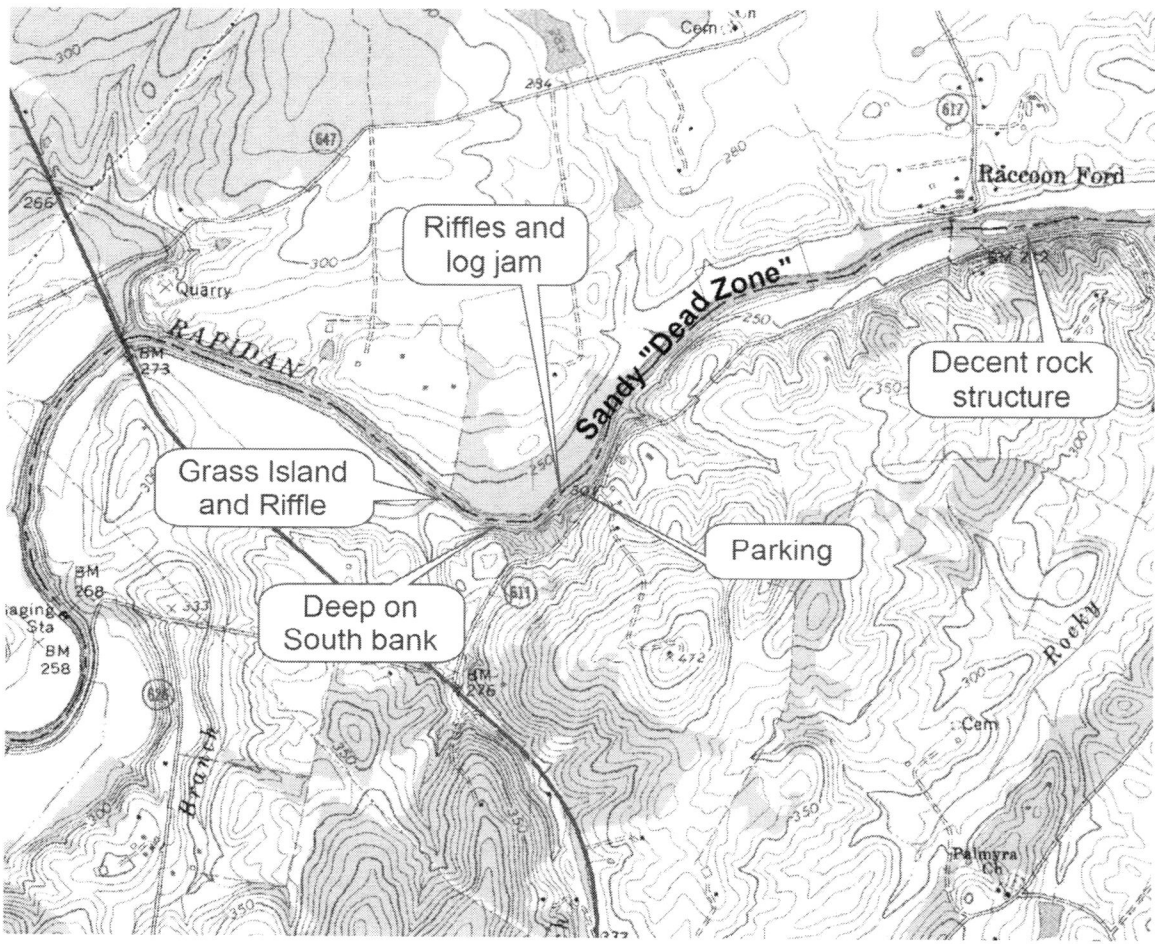

In general, the Rapidan is wide and slow throughout the entire Raccoon Ford section. You're hard-pressed to find any rock structure at all. In fact, the water runs slow enough to support a few largemouth bass in addition to smallmouth. There is barely enough structure to make this interesting to fish - and even then, you need to head in the right direction or totally waste your day.

Upstream

This is the last official VDGIF access point on the Rapidan. In the small, two car turnout, it explicitly states that parking is permitted only to launch canoes/kayaks or to fish. Once you walk down the narrow, very steep trail to get to the river, your first, and the best choice, to fish this section is to go upstream. A quick point on launching a boat - to get a canoe or kayak to the river will require a significant amount of manhandling. The trail twists and turns and will be slick if it's wet. You may just want to push your boat front in of you until it crashes into the water.

The trail to the river ends at a deep pool. If you make the mistake of entering the water there, you will quickly be up to your chest in water. Walk 10 feet upstream and enter from the rock ledge at the upstream boundary of the pool. From that perch, you can fish downstream into the pool and hit the deep spot since you did not spook the pool by entering. Turning upstream, there is nothing impressive or attractive. The river runs deep on the left-hand bank, shallow on the right where a sandbar provides a gradual ramp into the deeper section. It's easy wading throughout the entire upstream stretch as long as you stay to the center-right side of the river.

The best water to fish is between the entry point and the gradient break 500 feet upstream. As you walk up to the gradient break, concentrate on the channel that runs along the southern shoreline. I have never caught a smallmouth on the northern bank. There are randomly dispersed boulders providing the necessary structure to hold fish. To keep from wasting time, skip across the sandy sections unless you encounter a 4 foot or deeper pool. Once you reach the gradient break at 38.354433,-77.957209 , spend your time fishing both the up and downstream sections. Once done, walk another 150 feet to the sharp bend in the river. There is a particularly deep pool at that spot that holds largemouth bass and is worth fishing. Beyond that point, and around the bend, the deep channel continues along the southern bank all the way up to the large, grassy island (38.354256,-77.96084) that forms the upper boundary of your walk.

As you look upstream at the island, focus on the strong flow coming down the left-hand channel. You can pick up decent fish in the seams where it loses velocity. Don't bother to fish more than 50 feet above the island since the river turns into a sandy desert that runs most of the way up to the next access point.

Looking upstream from the access point, the deep channel is on the left-hand side.

The river runs wide, sandy and shallow into the bend.

Even at 140 cfs, there is not much to recommend in this location. Eventually, you walk up to this grassy complex.

You can fish the channel on the right-hand side of the deep pool created at the run-out on the left. But, it's a long walk to get to this water.

Be prepared to catch some largemouth bass in this area. The water is deep and quiet enough to allow them to grow to a fairly large size.

Downstream

I recommend against making the mistake of moving downstream.

But, that said, here's the description. Fish the deep hole where the trail joins the river. There is a good log complex directly across the river and that is where the fish will hold.

Beyond that spot, there is nothing good to say. There was an old dam at the informal access point that backed up the river for over a mile and allowed silt and sand to build up to excessive levels. While the dam is gone, the silt remains. It wiped out any decent habitat for smallmouth in this section. If you catch a bass here, it will be a rare event. On the other hand, if you like catching sunfish, have at it.

This is a place to fish once, learn your lesson and never return. In fact, I can't remember seeing a rock or a boulder anywhere in this entire stretch. Beyond the overhanging vegetation on the shoreline, there's nothing to attract and hold fish. Both shorelines are uniformly shallow and uninteresting. In doing the research for this book, I hiked approximately 600 yards downstream in search of productive water. Nothing!

Fish the log complex on the left that sits on the other side of the deep area next to the entry point.

I strongly recommend against walking downriver. It's shallow, sandy and totally dead.

Informal Access Point

Other authors discuss "informal" access points as being acceptable places to enter the river. As I mentioned in the discussion on regulations, these are typically beaten turnoffs at the edge of the river created by generations of anglers or others who use the river. The fact that they exist does not make access to the river from them legal. No matter how you cut it, unless there is a VDOT or other explicit easement from the road, **you will illegally cross private property to reach the water**. In the stretch of road to the west of the official access point, there used to be a very obvious informal access point at 38.361916,-77.941293 approximately 1,000 feet to the west of where Raccoon Ford Road joins the river. The landowner clearly did not appreciate people using this and has now piled a dirt berm along the previous entrance to restrict access.

I bring this up as an example of **where not to park.** The bad water continues all the way downstream from the official access point to the head of the old dam at the old informal access point. This access point is not on public land and you will cross over private property to reach the river. Since the fishing here is not anything to write home about, why bother?

If you stand at the edge of the road and look upstream from 38.361916,-77.941293, you can see the uniform brown color of the river bottom. Floating through here on a canoe, you can pick up some largemouth bass in the deep, although slow section 100 yards upstream of the island. At the old dam, you have two choices that are split by a large island across the river from the informal point. Go north or go south? Easy answer, beach your canoe at the sandy head of the island and wade the southern bank. If you take the northern channel, it leads into a shallow, sandy section that is not worth the energy. The only good spot to fish on the northern side is a deep pool at the base of the small gradient break that is the boundary between the backed up, silty area and the entrance. The southern channel, on the other hand, is better. It's full of good rocky structure with fast flowing water where the river picks up speed to compress through the narrow opening. It's easily wadeable if you stick to the shoreline of the island and hit the channel below the road. The good fishing ends at the eastern base of the island (38.362404,-77.936454) where the river duplicates the sandy character you saw upstream. If you want, you can walk another 50 yards downstream to where there is a small gradient break that spins into a deep pool on the left-hand side of the river. I do not recommend fishing any farther downstream than that point. Remember, private property lines both banks and the only place to leave the river is back at the official access point far upriver. Therefore, this spot is one for kayakers.

If you float down the river in a canoe, the riffle and subsequent water on the right-hand bank near the old informal (and illegal) access point is productive. Beach your canoe at the top of the island and wade downstream to take advantage of this.

Do not waste your time fishing down the left-hand side of the island. After fishing the initial channel that leads into a deep pool on the left, return to the top and work the more productive right-hand side.

Bottom Line

The strength of this spot is that it is a formally designated access point where you do not have to worry about landowners who may not understand the meaning of the VDOT right-of-way/easement at bridge crossings. Its weakness is that the "good" water is really not that good and only extends upstream, not down.

Route 522 Bridge

Google Map Coordinates: 38.358682,-77.97261

Summary Rating

Parking	Yellow	Spin Fishing	Green
Canoe/Kayak Launch	Green	Fly Fishing	Green
Distance to River	Green	Trout	Red
Can Bike to River	Red	Smallmouth Bass	Green
Physical Fitness	Green	Pressure	Green
Scenery	Yellow	Overall	Yellow

Green overall if you go upstream a mile. If you're not willing to make that long walk, this location drops to Yellow.

Special Regulations

There are no special fishing regulations in effect at this location.

Getting to the Stream

North: From Northern Virginia, take Exit 43B from I-66 onto US 29. Follow US 29 for 37 miles to the junction with US 522. Take the ramp from US 29 onto US 522 south. After 7 miles, US 522 crosses the bridge over the Rapidan. Go across the bridge and turn left into the gap between the highway and the fence to bump down the dirt-road to the unofficial parking area that is clearly visible on the Google satellite view (38.358682,-77.97261).

South: From I-64 in the Charlottesville area, take VA 231 north. Merge onto US 15 N followed by a right turn onto VA 20. Follow VA 20 until it intersects US 522. Follow US 522 north to the bridge.

Fishing here, as well as all the remaining places below the Shenandoah National Park, leverages the VDOT easement around bridges.

Environment and Fish

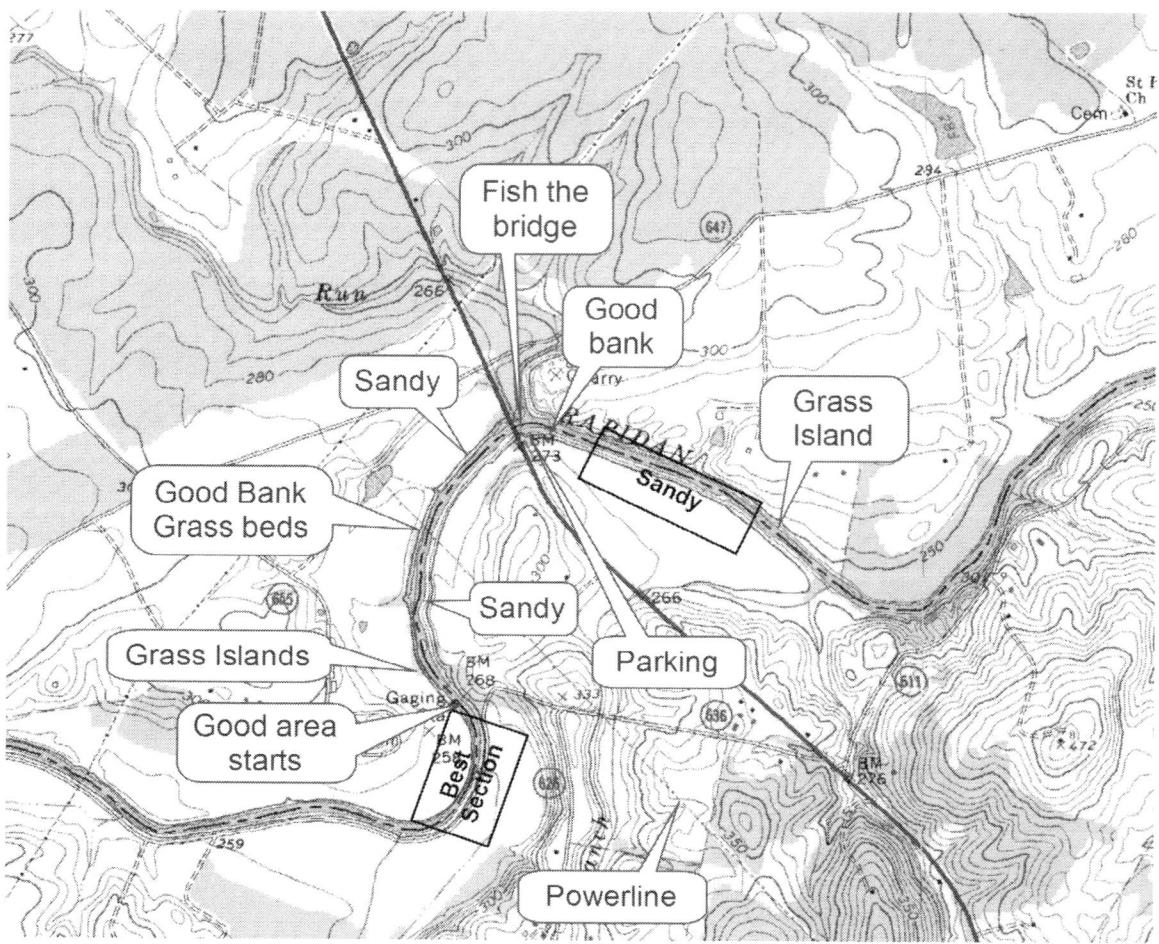

If you have low expectations, they will be met. At this point, the Rapidan is in the middle of a long, wide and gradually sloping valley. You should calibrate your hopes accordingly. The US 522 bridge is a popular put-in spot for canoes and kayaks. The broad, dirt road that leads from the highway into the small parking area shows evidence of extensive, heavy use over the years. Your initial look at the river will be favorable since it moves quickly underneath the bridge where it twists and turns around a small island complex to move downstream.

Upstream

To truly have a good day, you have to be willing to walk a mile upriver. Between the bridge and the riffle that is the landmark signaling the start of the good stretch, the smallmouth fishing is marginal.

As you enter the water underneath the bridge and look upstream, all you see is a desert. There are no rocks, just sand. In the middle the summer, at a gage reading of 228 cfs, the water is barely 2 feet deep. The deep section is on the right and you can pick up some sunfish underneath the log structure immediately upriver from the bridge. With nothing but sand in sight, you should skip this section but, if you do decide to fish here, target the shoreline structure with your attention informed by where the trees throw shade on the water. After the first two logjams on the right, fish the shaded bank to the left where it begins to run deep approximately hundred yards up from the bridge. There are two prominent fallen log structures on the left, opposite a narrow strip of grassy beds that are the home to as many sunfish as you care to pull in.

There are a few smallies in the upriver stretch and they are easy to find because they hold next to the structure. Since the river center is nothing but sand, fish to the edges where there are interesting logjams or shade. Finally, at 38.35740,-77.97513, the bottom changes to a mix of sand and small rocks. Don't get excited because this positive development is offset by the fact that it becomes even shallower than before; being less than a foot deep.

Continue to look to the shore instead of the center of the river. The grass beds on the right, while interesting to look at and tempting, push against a shallow shelf that will not hold any fish. At 38.35591,-77.97596, a set of power lines cross the river. Slow up as you approach that landmark. There is a deep hole underneath the fallen log structure and the overhanging tree just short of the power lines as well as a few randomly dispersed boulders on the downstream side next to the grass bed. There is a decent population of 12 inch smallmouth that live along the edge. Fish up and downstream of the power line; carefully throwing to both banks, but favoring one that has the most shade.

Above the power line, the river returns to its uniformly sandy character and retreats to being inches deep in the middle of summer. There is interesting structure up ahead and, if you have the energy, you may as well walk up and check it out. You need to be observant as you travel up the river and look for the clues of where the deep spots lie along the shore. A reliable indicator is to look for exposed tree roots. This only applies to large trees, but if the roots are massive and reach into the river, they create a swirl point that forces the water to scour out holes. These spots are always worth a cast.

The next landmark is the grassy island (38.35408,-77.97646) that splits the river approximately 0.6 miles upstream from the bridge. Fish the right bank immediately downstream of the island next to the overhanging tree and the long log that stretches parallel to the river. The main flow of the river is to the right of the island, but is not worth fishing since the river runs shallow and fast. However, upstream of the island, the river returns to the optimal rocky bottom with enough depth on the right-hand bank to make it worthwhile.

Cautiously wade above the island, fishing the right-hand bank up to the prominent rock on the right. The river narrows again with the main channel leaning right. Skip across the channel, unless the water is deep early in the season, by walking along the edge of the grassy shoreline. What lays in front of you is a wide expanse of the river with a shallow, sandy portion on the left and a deeper, shaded grass bed on the right. There are smallmouth in this small area. If there is any truth to the saying that 90% of the fish are in 10% of the river, then the lake below the island complies with that guidance.

Walk carefully to avoid spooking the fish in the shallow water and target the right-hand bank. You'll find the most fish upstream of the large dead stump that marks the start of the grass bed to the right. If you are here in the afternoon, concentrate on the edge of the grass bed where the shade protects it (38.35168,-77.97588). Once you catch one fish, stay there and work that spot since they pool up in the shaded areas to avoid the heat. Slowly, slowly work your way up the grass bed as this is the key spot that holds the fish in the mile that you walked upstream. Float small poppers, size 8 or 10, along the weeds and you'll have plenty of action. At 38.35121,-77.97539, the river takes a sharp downward plunge and runs over a 50 yard, 2 inch deep stretch of shallow riffles. Above the riffle, there is an old bridge piling - it is 0.94 miles from the US 522 bridge.

You now have to face a pretty tough decision. Continue or go back? Upriver, the river bed transitions from sand to rock and small stones. If you want to go farther upstream, move to the right-hand bank. At a gage reading of 200 cfs and above, it's too deep in the center. That depth will be an absolute joy to encounter after dealing with the shallow water in the 1 mile hike to get here. The farther upstream you go, the more the river bottom moves away from sand into rock. If you have the energy to fish upstream of the bridge, this is the holy grail you are looking for.

The next 150 yards is infested with smallmouth. Between the bridge piling and the next set of rocks marking a gradient break upstream, the river holds at 3 to 4 feet transitioning to 1 to 2 feet at the break. VA 636 parallels the river at this point and if you get into trouble, you can find a place to climb out. The bank next the road is steep with limited opportunities for escape -- but at least it's an option. Recognize that the bank is private property - exit is for emergencies only. Do not make the mistake of thinking you can walk on the road back to your vehicle. If you do that, you will add a mile to your return trip. It's better to gut it out and walk in the river back to the bridge. Speaking of the road, if you can get within casting distance of all of the rocks that line the left-hand bank and support the roadway, you can exploit the deep channel that hugs the bank.

As you go around the corner, stay to the right to get by the deepest area. Once through that difficult spot, move towards the center of the river as far you can go. The water remains deep for the next 100 yards and you may as well walk in the center and fish both banks. Which bank gets your attention will depend on how much sun there is on the water and where the trees throw the shade. You will have to move back and forth to find wadeable passage upstream to the next riffle break. I prefer to stay on the right-hand bank because the left-hand bank is unvaryingly steep as a result of the road. Although the river returns to a sand-mud bottom approximately 200 yards up from the bridge piling, the depth allows the smallies to range freely. The landmark indicating the return to a rocky bottom with a minimum of sand is a huge tree on the right-hand bank that has fallen parallel to the river.

At the gradient break that marks my recommended upper bound, the depth is only a foot and a half at normal summer levels. The grass beds on the right are not really productive; being shallow in the summer. Instead, the main depth of the river runs from the center to the right-hand bank.

Once you reach the gradient break at 38.34785,-77.97473, you are 1.25 miles from the bridge. That's a long walk back, so consider that before you make your choice to hump all the way upriver.

You will be totally "bummed out" when you take your first step into the river and look upstream. It's nothing but sand and shallow water – even at 135 cfs.

Walk quickly up to the power line (shown here) and fish the grass bed on the right-hand side. There's a good channel that runs up the bank for about 30 yards.

Beyond the power line, you encounter better, rocky structure with interesting grass lining each side.

Don't expect anything big here. Most of the guys you catch will be this size.

This is the shallow riffle leading down from the piling that marks the start of the optimum section. The piling is on the left-hand side of the picture.

There is a small backup of water created by the piling that represents the start of the exceptional fishing. You are a mile from the bridge at this point.

The river shallows as it moves around the turn upstream from the pilings. The grass structure on the left and the trees on the right are both good.

This gradient break and associated rock structure represents the upstream limit.

Downstream

After you fish the water directly under the bridge, the deep pool continues downstream on the right-hand bank. The overhanging vegetation that clusters along the shoreline provides plenty of shade as well as opportunities for ants and grasshoppers to drop into the river. In fact, it's fairly deep on the shoreline and you need to move out into the river from the island to the right of the bridge. Walk down the center of the river and target the bank. The good fishing continues for 300 feet downstream of the bridge through a short complex of gradient breaks that feature plenty of rocks and other structure.

Don't hurry as you fish the area around the bridge because this is the only good water in the downstream direction. The fast, good water runs from 38.358877,-77.971762 to 38.358692,-77.970955. Continue below the last ridge of rocks and fish both shorelines downstream for 100 feet to take advantage of the tree structure next to the bank. While not deep, the water is deep enough. Beyond that, the river turns into a desert -- a dead zone. The next 1,200 yards are a waste of time.

If you insist on going farther downstream just to prove it to yourself, walk quickly to the next small area of rocks that occurs at 38.357676,-77.967567 followed by another marginal area at 38.357026,-77.965483. Fish those and don't expend any additional energy. It's a long, hard slog back up to the bridge since the water is consistently a foot or more deep and constantly conspires to drag your feet downriver; pulling you back to some of the worst fishing on the river.

There is a deep channel that runs from the bridge around the tip of the sandy peninsula shown here.

The deep channel parallels the right-hand bank. Pay attention to the deep water underneath the trees at the right of this picture.

This is a picture of the wasted 1,200 yards at 140 cfs.

This is another view of the dead 1,200 yards from the grassy islands that mark the downstream boundary of that waste of time.

Bottom Line

You might conclude from the above discussion that the US 522 bridge crossing is one to totally write off. Instead, you should look at this as a stop on a longer day of fishing. It's decent in the area around the bridge. So, why not fish there and then move on someplace else? You definitely do not want to expend an entire day in this section unless you're willing to wade a mile upstream. If you can do that, the game changes and this spot becomes attractive.

Rapidan Dam

Google Map Coordinates: 38.310279,-78.065715

Summary Rating

Parking	Yellow	Spin Fishing	Green
Canoe/Kayak Launch	Green	Fly Fishing	Green
Distance to River	Green	Trout	Red
Can Bike to River	Red	Smallmouth Bass	Green
Physical Fitness	Green	Pressure	Yellow
Scenery	Red	Overall	Yellow

The populated area, limited parking and a requirement to obtain a pass add up to the overall rating of Yellow.

Special Regulations

Well, maybe. Elsewhere in this book, I discuss the VDOT easement around bridge crossings and streambed ownership. The first time I came here, I leveraged that authority to reach the water underneath the bridge where I saw this sign painted on one of the pilings.

What gives? I called the number and spoke with a very nice person who told me the company that owns the land around the bridge is happy to issue free fishing passes to anyone who requests one. Rather than push the issue with VDGIF, I sent her my information and received the pass back. It was a painless process and I recommend you do the same instead of getting into an argument at the river's edge. The form you need to send is at the end of this chapter.

Getting to the Stream

From US 29 in Culpeper, take the ramp to US 522/VA 3 E (Germanna Highway). Stay on US 522 and turn right on VA 615 (Rapidan Road). Follow VA 615 to Rapidan and turn right to go to the bridge. There is a very small (1-2 car) parking area to the left immediately before crossing the bridge. You can also park farther down the road near the old train station and walk back up.

Canoe/Kayak Comment: To describe the parking area as limited is an understatement. If you are lucky, a spot will be empty and you can unload your gear and drop it into the water. If not, you may have to pull off on the right-hand side of the road facing southwest, drop your gear and move your vehicle back down the road to the old train station. It's a short, easy walk down the path to get to the river's edge.

Environment and Fish

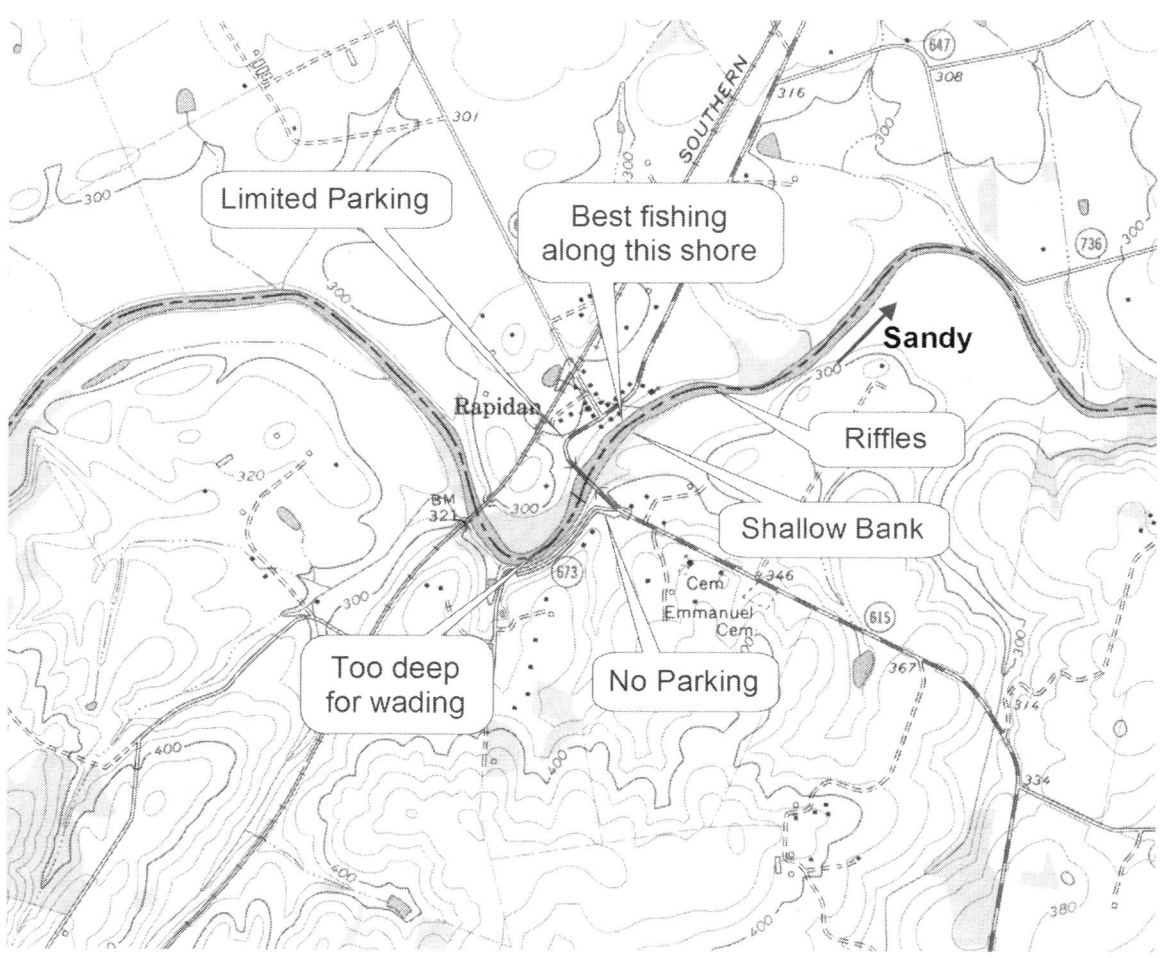

After being put off a bit by the sign, I returned with my pass tucked safely in my fishing vest and walked purposefully down to the river. There is only one direction to fish since the dam is the prominent terrain feature upstream. Above the dam, the water is deep and full of mud. If you cross to the east side of the river and turn right onto VA 673, it parallels the river for approximately 800 feet until it veers away to the south. Don't bother to look for access along that shoreline. The dam creates a lake that extends 900 feet upstream that prevents wading. Even if it was wadeable, there is no place to park. The access pass specifically prohibits parking in the small lot adjacent to the building on the east side of the river.

In addition, do not get aggressive and walk down the railroad tracks from Locust Dale Road to intersect the river a little farther upstream from the dam. All railroad property in Virginia is automatically classified as posted.

The good news is that this is a first-rate fishing location. Once on the river, point your rod upstream and wade into the area below the dam to the extent the water levels will permit. It's a dense complex full of rocks and cuts that offers good fishing.

When you're done, turn downstream and move to the center of the river via the sloping sandbar on the right-hand bank. The deep channel is on the left-hand bank with tall, overhanging trees that throw considerable shade over the deep area; making it a perfect place for big fish to hold in the heat of the summer. The deep run continues past the houses that dominate the left-hand bank. Put aside your jealousy that they sit on such great water and take advantage of the fact that you can reach it from the sandbar.

Just beyond the houses, the river changes from good to bad. The rocks disappear and the sand begins, but you only have to deal with the sand for 400 feet. At the bend in the river, a peninsula (38.313627,-78.061839) sticks out from the left that compresses the flow over a gradient break. The constriction causes the velocity of the water to increase and scour the bottom; revealing another rocky section. Stand on the end of the peninsula and fish the deep hole on the left. The deep water holds on both sides of the river, so you must move along a high ridgeline in the center of the river. You should take your time between here and the downstream gradient break at 38.313555,-78.060128. This is 400 feet of pretty good fishing with decent numbers of rocks and other attractive structure to make it interesting for smallmouth.

Sadly, at the second gradient break, the river flips back to sand from gravel. You can continue to target some deep areas farther downstream, but this should be the limit of your walk. Head back to the bridge and call it a day.

There is usually a decent amount of water as a result of the dam on the other side of the bridge.

At 362 cfs, the river is full but still wadeable using the sandbar to the right. The productive bank is on the left under the trees.

At higher water levels, you'll be closed out as you approach the left-hand bank. The water gets extremely deep and the only way to reach it is from the sandbar in the center.

Beyond the houses, the river returns to rock and shallows out as it runs into the turn.

This picture and the one to the right show the water below the riffle.

It is productive underneath the trees on the left.

Bottom Line

Get your pass and take advantage of this section of the river. There are enough rocks and deep water to hold some monsters. Focus on the area close to the dam for the best results. The farther you walk downstream, the worse the water becomes.

Here is the permission form. Follow the directions to get the pass. It does not expire so you can keep it with your fishing tackle and use it forever.

**FPC Inc
704 Locust Avenue
Charlottesville, Virginia 22903
434-979-8900
434-979-8901 (Fax)**

For: Rapidan Fishing Club

Thank you for your interest in fishing at Rapidan Mill.

Please find enclosed a short form to fill out and be returned to our office, with a ***self-addressed stamped envelope*** (to receive your approved application); we will sign it, make a copy for our records and return it to you quickly. Without an envelope and stamp we will be unable to return your application.

You may also fax it to us if you prefer and we can fax it back. **Please feel free to make as many copies as you need.**

**RAPIDAN FISHING CLUB APPLICATION
C/O FPC Inc
704 Locust Avenue • Charlottesville, VA 22902
434-979-8900 • 434-979-8901 (Fax)**

Name: _____

Address: _____

Phone: _____

Car: Year: _____ Make: _____ Model: _____

License Plate: _____ State: _____

RULES:
1. Any activity on this property is at your own risk.
2. Clean up after yourself; do not leave trash on this property. Any trash receptacles on this land are NOT for member use. Take your trash with you.
3. **This signed Membership Application DOES NOT give you permission to park on our property or any adjoining property.**

I have read and understand the above rules and agree to abide by them. I agree to have this letter on my person when on Rapidan Mill Property along with proof of identification.

Signature: _____ Date: _____

Rapidan Mill LLC/FPC Agent Signature: _____ Date: _____

Madison Mills (US 15)

Google Map Coordinates: 38.280909,-78.139529

Summary Rating

Parking	**Green**	Spin Fishing	**Green**
Canoe/Kayak Launch	**Green**	Fly Fishing	**Green**
Distance to River	**Green**	Trout	**Red**
Can Bike to River	**Red**	Smallmouth Bass	**Green**
Physical Fitness	**Green**	Pressure	**Green**
Scenery	**Green**	Overall	**Green**

Even though the fishing upstream is limited based on the lake that occurs soon after you point your rod in that direction, the overall experience is good.

Special Regulations

There are no special fishing regulations in effect at this location.

Getting to the Stream

North: From Culpeper, take US 15 south until you reach the river. Immediately prior to the river, turn west on VA 659 and follow the road to the parking area near the bridge.

South: From I-64, take exit 136 for US 15 towards Gordonsville. At the traffic circle, stay on US 15N. Once you cross the river, turn left onto VA 659 and follow it the short-distance to the river.

The road that leads to the medium-sized parking area is actually the old road that existed prior to opening the four-lane highway. Be thankful that it has been left in place since it provides plenty of parking. After you park, walk to the end of the road to discover the obvious, well beaten trail that leads to the river. Stay on the path since the land to the west is posted.

Canoe/Kayak comments: It's an easy walk down the narrow path to drop your boat into the water. There is plenty of space in the parking area to sort out your gear.

Environment and Fish

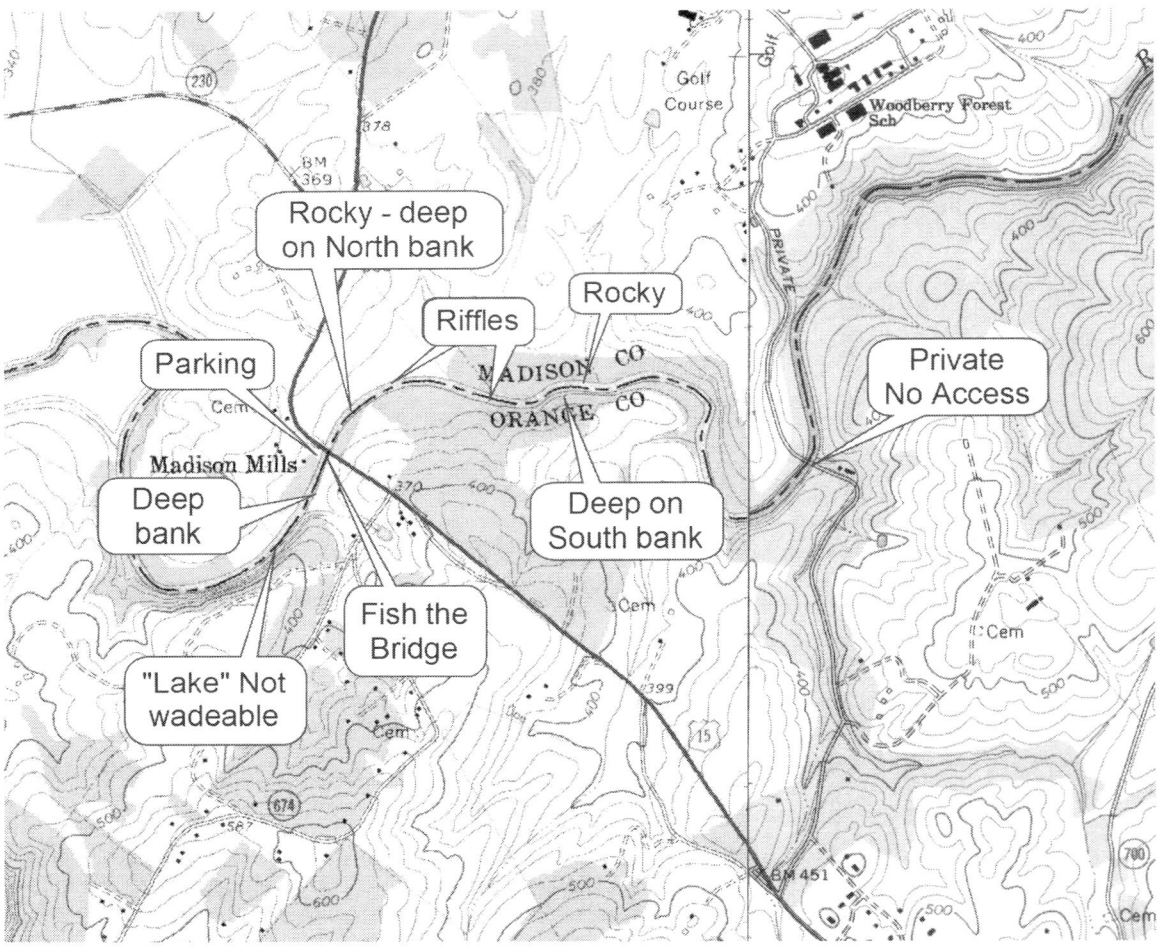

This is a good spot. There is a lake a short distance upstream that will close you out, but the downstream run offers decent smallmouth structure that supports a good day of fishing.

Upstream

This is another place where you should begin fishing as soon as you set foot in the river because:

1. The section immediately downstream of the parking lot is deep, fast and offers good structure
2. It closes out 50 yards upstream on a wide, deep lake that stretches from bank to bank. Since your only access is below the low water mark as a result of private property on both sides, you are forced to remain in the river. Unless you are willing to swim or paddle your way upstream, your day is done when you hit the lake.

Immediately upon reaching the edge of the river, tie on the appropriate lure and fish the deep pool that marks the boundary between the path and the bridge. It's shallow on the near bank so you can walk out into the river to get everywhere you need to go.

After plumbing the depths, wade out and direct your attention to the deep hole that is immediately to the right front and at the tail end of a tangle of fallen logs piled up on the other side of the river. This is a target rich environment! Fish through the tangle and turn back to the right-hand bank to hit the fast run that clings to the shoreline and is sheltered by the overhanging trees. In short, the entire area around the trailhead deserves a decent amount of your time.

The next landmark is upstream. There is a grassy, sandy island that divides the river into two channels. Cautiously approach the downstream end; throwing into the seams of the current on either side. The more productive side is the right-hand bank where the river sweeps underneath dense, protruding vegetation that creates a shady refuge. Don't ignore the smaller channel on the left-hand side or the pool at its head. At a minimum, you can pick up some massive sunfish along with medium-sized smallmouth. Once done with the edges, fish the deep pool immediately downstream of the island.

Move to the top of the island and fish the tail end of the lake. The left-hand bank is the best one to target as far as you can wade upstream. Unfortunately, it's fairly deep and that limits your ability to make any forward progress. There is rock structure underneath the water so use lures that go deep to drag up the big smallmouth that live along the edge. You may be able to squeeze by on the right-hand side, but you will find it to be exceptionally muddy and slippery. Definitely do not try and circumnavigate the lake if you are wearing waders because you are certain to slip and end up in the water.

After fishing upstream as far you can, turn your attention to the other side of the bridge. Even though you cannot fish very far upstream, you can penetrate as far downstream as you have the energy to do so.

Sorry for the dark picture, but you can still make out all of the "posted" signs to the right of the trail. Be sure you respect private property.

Once on the river, the view upstream reveals some fast-moving water with good channels terminating in some grass islands.

The area just downstream of the grass island is deep and holds good numbers of decent size smallmouth.

On the way to the grass islands, carefully cover this twisted group of logs.

Unfortunately, above the grass island is nothing but lake.

From the left-hand side of the river, the view confirms that the deep water continues around the bend upstream.

Downstream

Undoubtedly, you will fish the deep hole that leads into the bridge. Although the river flips from rock to mud and sand at this point, the depth compensates and fish collect around the bridge. In fact, the depth will surprise you if you became used to the shallow water that exists in most of the other areas of the Rapidan. Wade around the deep section by holding tight to the bridge pylons on the right-hand side of the river. It is a muddy slog - so be careful if you are wearing waders that you do not slip into the deep water. At times, you can sink in the mud up to your knee, so stay as close to the low water mark as you can.

Once past the bridge, the river bottom returns to the "smallmouth friendly" mix of rock and sand running about 2 feet deep when the flow is 400 cfs. Stay to the right hand side of the river and pay careful attention to the overhanging structure stretching all the way to the bend. Although the water underneath the trees is shallow, fish hold there in the heat of the day. The river runs deeper on the left-hand side as it goes into the bend; making it worth walking down the middle of the river and throwing to both banks. Since the river is not wide, you can work both sides at the same time.

The closer you get to the bend in the river, the deeper it gets on the left; culminating underneath the hanging rope that denotes a local swimming hole. Stay to the right and continue to fish down the bank. Although the river shallows out approximately one hundred yards downstream from the bridge, the structure is compelling and you can pick up fish when the water levels allow for a decent amount of depth. The river maintains its mix of rock and sand all the way down to the bend.

Once past the bend where the swimming hole is, the river shallows out; returning to a depth of between 1 and 2 feet running over a flat rock shelf. The shelf has a small amount of gravel as well as a few large boulders to break up the monotony. This continues down to the gradient break at the next bend. Fish each boulder carefully.

At the bend, there is good rock structure that reaches all the way across the river (38.282345,-78.136289). Fish the downstream tail of the pools created near the boulders as well as the lead into the gradient break itself.

When you approach the gradient, be aware that the deep section is in the middle of the river. The bottom continues to be speckled with boulders and shallows out at the edges. Make a choice of either going along the right or left bank and fish the middle. It's good from either direction.

At this point, you are at 38.28246,-78.13646. Looking downstream, the water shallows again all the way down to the tree leaning precipitously over the river on the right-hand side. You may be inclined to skip this stretch, but there is a good pool that holds large sunfish to the left of the rock jetty on the left edge of the river.

Continue to fish the deep section on the left-hand side. There's another rock ledge that stretches across the river next to where a blowdown and sandbar create a deep pool on the downstream side. Approach that great structure with caution and fish the deep pool from upstream.

Stay on river left because the depth is now on the right-hand bank. The closer you get to the next bend, the deeper the river becomes as it goes into the left-hand turn. As you approach the bend, it transitions through a sandy stretch that ends at a beaver dam next to a rope swing hanging from a large tree. Thankfully, the river returns to its rocky structure at the bend and continues into the distance. Since, at this point, you are approximately 0.75 miles from the parking lot and should head back because your return hike will be a tough fight against the water pushing downstream against your waterlogged boots. Be sure you have plenty of energy before you move this far downstream.

Below the trailhead, the river forms a deep pool. I prefer to get around it on the right-hand bank.

Fish under the bridge in the deep water.

The downstream perspective at 240 cfs is good. Plenty of fishable water.

Focus on the trees that throw shade on the water!

Up and downstream of each ripple is good.

A rope hung from a tree means deep water. Good to know in the summer when the bass go deep to escape the heat.

The river turns sandy leading into the bend.

This is the turnaround point.

Bottom Line

Either direction ends up being pretty good. Go upstream for a short, quick fishing trip or beat your way downstream to the rock structure that will hold smallmouth for a full day of sport.

Liberty Mills (Route 231)

Google Map Coordinates: 38.231316,-78.21991

Summary Rating

Parking	Red	Spin Fishing	Green
Canoe/Kayak Launch	Yellow	Fly Fishing	Green
Distance to River	Green	Trout	Red
Can Bike to River	Red	Smallmouth Bass	Green
Physical Fitness	Green	Pressure	Yellow
Scenery	Yellow	Overall	Red

The sandy bottom and lack of rocky structure push the overall rating to Red. There are some rocky channels upstream, but they are not compelling enough to make this a day trip. Most of the other people you encounter will be swimming underneath the bridge.

Special Regulations

There are no special fishing regulations in effect at this location.

Getting to the Stream

North: From US 29 at Culpeper, turn south on US 15 S (Orange Road). Turn right at West Main Street and continue onto VA 20 S (Constitution Highway). Turn right onto VA 231 (Blue Ridge Turnpike) and follow it to the bridge.

South: From I-64, take exit 136 for US 15 towards Gordonsville. At the traffic circle, turn onto US 33 W/VA 231 N (North Main Street). Follow VA 231 to the bridge.

There are two places to park on the south side of the bridge. On the west side, there's a small two car informal parking area and on the east side there is a wide spot at the intersection of VA 231 with VA 641.

Canoe/Kayak comment: While the river is close to where you can park, the portage is a little longer and requires negotiating across the typical large boulders that support a major bridge.

Environment and Fish

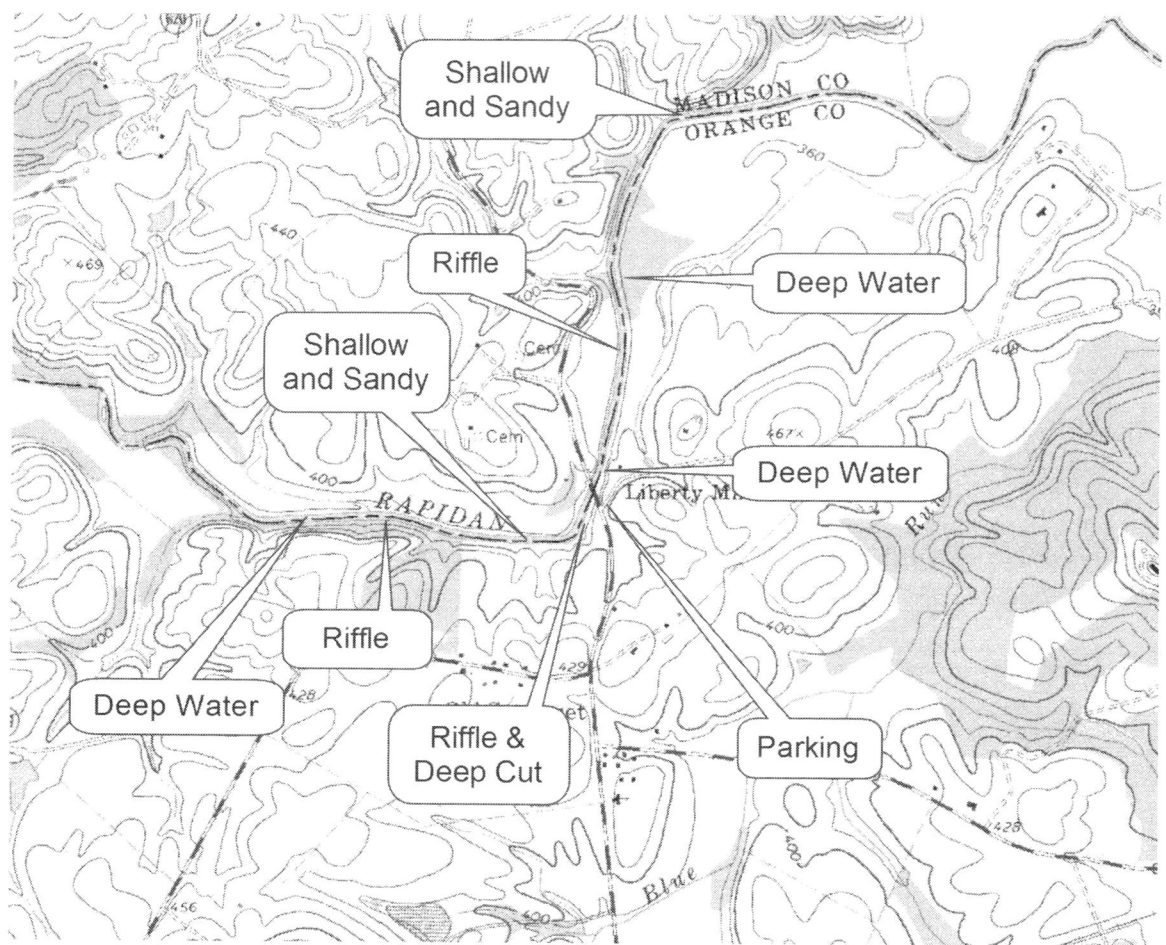

Upstream

After fishing under the bridge, move upstream into the rock garden. There's no clear path on one side of the river or the other to get through. As you fish the cuts that create the maze, you'll find yourself moving from the left bank to the right and back again to move upstream. Pay extra attention to the deeper hole to the right of the tall rock (38.230347,-78.220572). Move to the right bank, head upriver and fish the cut created as the river runs around the bend.

After fishing the bend, walk upstream to the gradient break (38.230296,-78.225271). Be comfortable skipping everything between the bend and the break because it's a mix of sand giving way to a cobbled, rocky bottom. If you feel like it, fish the tail pool where the river turns to the south to make a small corner and run down a steep bank. Another spot to fish is the pool at the head of the break on river right. However, these tend to dry up in the summer and I doubt you will catch anything other than sunfish.

As you fish your way up the lake that backs up at the head of the break, concentrate on the left. In particular, fish the two small cliff faces that border a large overhanging tree. It gets between 5 and 7 feet deep in that spot and fish hold there. Eventually, if the water is high enough, you'll be closed out and have to move to the right to walk along the edge of the river and cross over a large fallen tree to get back better water.

At that point, the lake continues and it is worthwhile fishing on the left because of all of the overhanging trees and structure. The riverbed gradually turns from sand back to a mix of rock and sand leading up to the next gradient break (38.23076, -78.22792) where the river takes a slight turn to the right (looking upstream). Above the break, there's a good run along several fallen logs on the right. Fish the run and move into the next lake area staying on the left (the shallow side) where you can fish the overhanging brush that leans off the high bank on the right. Continue slowly up; terminating at the next small gradient break; be sure and fish the boulder just downstream of the break.

At that point, you are 0.65 miles from the bridge. What's ahead of you is more of the same - a mostly sandy bottom with overhanging brush and a few logs. The smallies will be few and far between in this type of habitat and you should turn around and trudge back to the bridge.

The short section upstream of the bridge has smallmouth friendly rocky structure.

There is a deep pool on the left at the bend above the rocks.

The area near the next bend is also good.

Beyond that, it's a boring mix of sand and shallow water.

There is one interesting spot on the right where the sandbar pushes the water into a deeper channel.

Don't go any farther since it's only sand.

Downstream

As you wade into the water at the bridge and face downstream, there is not much to generate excitement since the bottom is solid sand. The redeeming feature is that there are deep sections downstream that attract fish. At 38.23539, -78.21888 (0.4 miles down from the bridge), the river switches from sand to rock as it enters the first gradient break. It's not worth fishing the headwater since it is unusually shallow. Fish the deep stretch below the tree that has fallen across the river. Skip the section inside the break and move downstream to the end of the fast water where there is a hole on the right. Fish the spot on the left where a large bush leans out into the river. At the bottom of the second break, the river pools up on the left.

Move slowly down on the right and fish the left-hand bank. Let your lure sink all the way to the bottom for the best results. After you spend the appropriate amount of time, turn your attention to the lake that stretches downstream for approximately 100 yards. Don't hurry through this area because this is the first place you will encounter a substantial number of smallmouth.

Fish your way down the lake as far you can -- you will eventually become closed out by the deep water. The farthest you may want to walk is to 38.23858, -78.21933. That point is 0.62 miles from the bridge and represents a good hike through water that is moderately deep at normal levels. If you come here at low water levels, you may be able to go a little bit farther. The obstacle that impedes progress is the deep, very soft mud that packs the bank. After you sink into the silt and fight your way down a few yards, you will conclude that further movement downstream is not worth the effort.

Even if you press on, at low water, the streambed at the tail end of the lake turns back to solid sand and becomes shallow and unproductive as it runs down a gentle gradient producing a small rapids. That condition persists downstream to 38.24124, -78.21815. The bottom line is that the effort to move beyond the lake is not worth it. It's just a long walk back for not a lot of results.

If you are compelled by the need to see new water, you may set a goal of wading down the river all the way to the sharp right-hand turn at 38.24244, -78.21713. Don't. I have and the river stays muddy and shallow as it goes around the corner.

Fish under the bridge.

Downstream, the deep water is on the right.

The river is featureless.

The view upstream is equally boring.

Eventually, the river shallows out, turns rocky and runs through a gradient break that produces ripples at the bend. Fish above and below this section for best results.

The lead into the bend also has some decent water.

Bottom Line

Not a great place, but not horrible. Downstream is better than up and you may just want to fish the area in the immediate vicinity of the bridge if you get here before the swimmers show up .

Ruckersville (US 29)

Google Map Coordinates: 38.279957,-78.341387

Summary Rating

Parking	Yellow	Spin Fishing	Green
Canoe/Kayak Launch	Green	Fly Fishing	Green
Distance to River	Green	Trout	Red
Can Bike to River	Red	Smallmouth Bass	Green
Physical Fitness	Yellow	Pressure	Yellow
Scenery	Green	Overall	Green

There is a decent amount of parking directly under the bridge. While upstream is the better choice, it also puts you in contact with more rocky structure; making it a little more challenging physically.

Special Regulations

There are no special fishing regulations in effect at this location.

Getting to the Stream

North: From Culpeper, head south on US 29 until you cross the river. Make a U-turn and take the dirt road to the east of the highway to the small parking area next to the bridge.

South: From Charlottesville, go north on US 29 until you approach the river. Turn off onto the small dirt road to the east of the highway that bumps down into the small parking area next to the bridge.

I recommend you not follow the dirt road when it veers right since the track clearly moves away from the easement onto private property. Another caution is not to follow what appears to be a dim track beyond the hard packed dirt to the area under the bridge. It leads to marshland... hidden under a layer of grass that will sink your vehicle up to the axles if you go too far.

In fact, once you park and are on foot, do not follow the trail that leads under the bridge since that puts you in the middle of a big mud hole. Instead go straight to the river; staying to the right of the marshy area. Once you reach the river, follow the beaten trail under the bridge to move upstream or just start fishing downstream.

Canoe/Kayak comment: This is an easy place to launch. It has a sandy bank and the parking area is only feet away from the river.

Environment and Fish

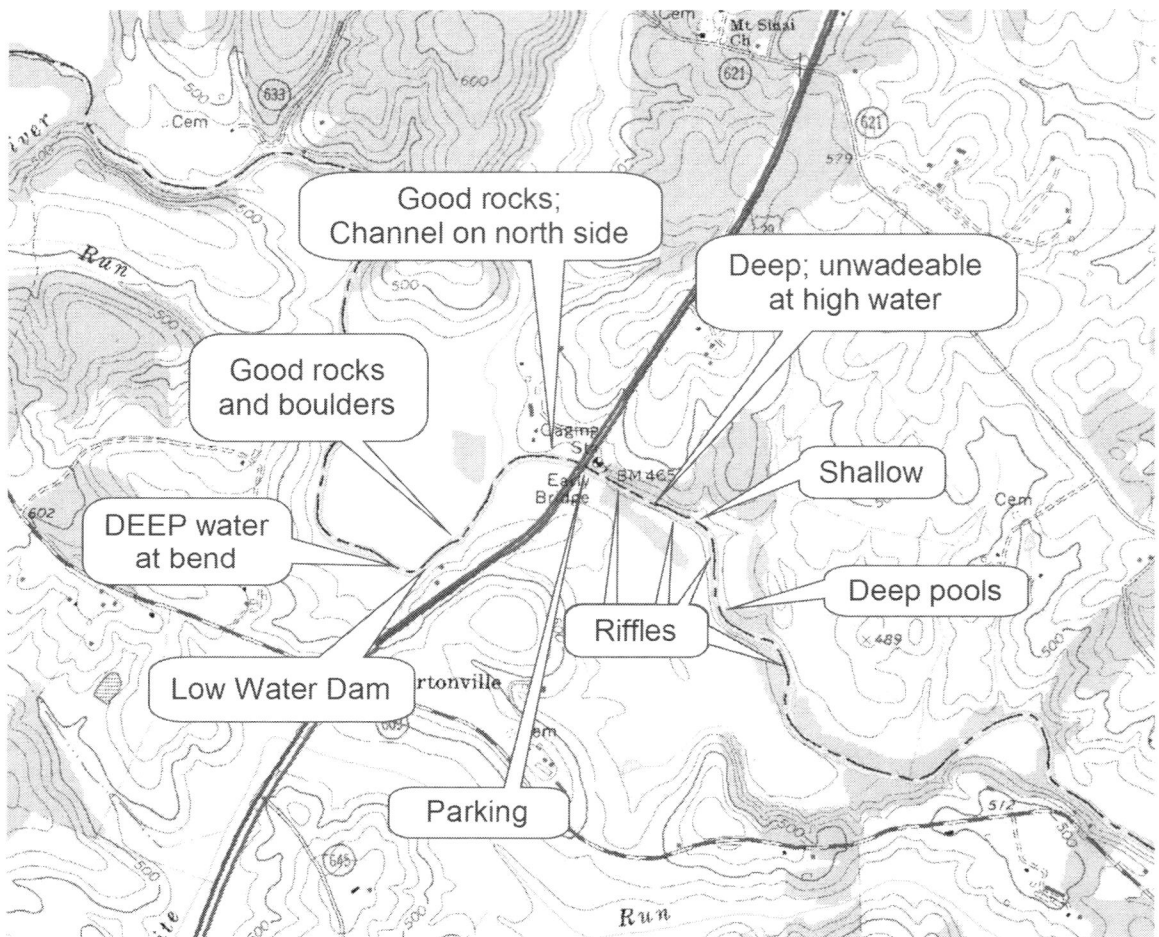

Upstream

Begin fishing immediately at the bridge; focusing on the right bank. There's a good, fast cut that runs over a pockmarked, rocky bottom with a perpendicular ledge immediately upstream from the bridge. Continue to head upstream and concentrate on the right bank until the water gets skinny in the middle of the gradient break. By the time you get up to the corner at 38.28025,-78.34297, you should have caught a couple decent size smallies and as many sunfish as you care to pull in.. At the corner, the river changes to wide and shallow with a slower push; making it easier to move upstream.

After running shallow for 25 to 30 yards, the river takes a hard left around the bend to become uniformly 2 to 3 feet deep early in the summer. With good rock structure on the bottom, this area holds a decent population of smallmouth as well as sunfish. The deeper section is towards the center, so choose one side or the other to walk up and cast to the middle. By late June or early July, this will shallow out. After running shallow for 50 yards, there is a dramatic plunge in depth and it can be up to 6 feet deep near 38.27900,-78.34447. Look for a cluster of fallen logs on the right to see where the significant transition occurs. Move to the left and wade on that side. Although it can be 3 to 4 feet deep early in the summer, you can make it if you have chest waders on or if you are wet wading and don't care how deep the water gets (PFD!). After the deep section, the rock and cobble bottom disappears and sand, interspersed with rocks and boulders, reappears. There are large boulders spread throughout the subsequent 50 yard long pool. Fish on either side of each boulder. Deep in the summer, the shallow edge will begin to look like a long rocky beach.

Have a popper tied on when you reach the end of the pool to be ready for the glorious rock structure that lays in front of you. The sand disappears and is replaced by a dense boulder field that provides plenty of protected holes - fish up either bank.

By the time you reach 38.27713,-78.34664, a low water dam, your arms should be sore from all the fish! Take it easy on the shallow stretch. It is worth throwing at the fallen log on the right if the water is deep enough, but you should probably jump to the pool below the low water dam. At the dam, there is a low water bridge that ends your wading experience. Beyond the dam, the water backs up and prevents further movement upstream except by clinging to the right-hand bank and slogging through the mud. If it is safe to do so, be sure and fish the pools on either side of the dam. In fact, you can stand on the low water dam and fish the deep pool downstream for an hour. There are hordes of sunfish and smallies lurking in the deep water; waiting for food to wash across the top of the dam.

If you are here on a day when you can wade above the dam, it's worth going to the large, deep hole carved by the water at the next bend (38.27706,-78.34752). At normal water levels, it could be as much as 15 feet deep. Above the pool, the river takes a hard left against a starkly cut dirt bank. This is the second place where access will be cut off - it's just not possible to wade and stay within the confines of the river, avoiding private property, beyond this point.

Start fishing as soon as you head upstream from the bridge. The right-hand bank has the deep channel.

The view downstream into the bend shows random, scattered rocks.

The drop in elevation at the bend creates a small lake upstream. Continue to focus on the right-hand bank and move gradually to the left.

The next pitch of the river is all good smallmouth habitat with a solid rocky bottom consisting of medium-size stones. There are no defined channels, look for the boulders to find the fish.

Farther upstream, the water deepens and forces you to either bank to continue upriver. At 309 cfs, this is still wadeable.

There is a brief sandy section downstream of the medium-sized island that splits the river below the low water dam.

This picture and the one to the right demonstrate the dynamic nature of the river. Note that the river, above the dam, is clear in this shot.

A few months later, the leaning tree had fallen just above the low water dam. Stay to the left to wade up to the dam and fish the very deep water to the right.

Above the dam, at the bend in the river, the water is 10 to 15 feet deep.

The bend is as far as you can go and not violate private property. The river remains deep as it crashes against the red dirt bank.

Downstream

There's no reason not to start fishing immediately under the bridge. It contains a deep hole that stretches all the way to the rocks 100 yards downstream at 38.279706,-78.340121 (Riffle #1). The smallies will be throughout this stretch and concentrated in the area as a result of the good bottom structure. After the first 100 yards, the bottom switches to random boulders with a few rocks surrounded by sand. If the water is high, you may be closed out about halfway down to the second gradient break at 38.278823,-78.338056 (Riffle #2).

At normal summer levels, you will not have any problem getting all the way down. As you walk downstream, fish the left bank where the overhanging structure throws some shade on the water. The right bank is basically a dead zone once you get beyond the first 50 yards. At riffle #2, there are number of good boulders just upstream of the rocks that poke their noses above the surface of the water. Downstream, the gradient break forces the water into a fast, shallow run that extends for approximately 100 yards. A half mile downstream at 38.27723, -78.33618, the river takes a hard right turn and runs through a tight corner where the water speeds up as it compresses between the narrow banks. Fish the deep turn. At the other end of the gradient break, the water runs out into another long flat lake.

Once past the deep spots by the turn, move to the left and fish the right-hand bank. Be sure to fish the submerged structure after moving left. The deep stretch on the right continues downstream to the rock and gravel sandbar in the distance. Beyond that, there's a small drop in elevation creating a pool on the right that will be your next target. At lower water levels, you should skip directly to that spot.

Around the corner on the other side of the sandbar, there is a huge hole underneath a tall bushy tree. It's probably 10 or 15 feet deep and demands significant attention. It's a perfect place to float a popper;

twitching it gently underneath the low hanging branches. After hitting the deep hole at the tree, walk down to the next bend in the river. The intervening river, while rocky, runs fairly shallow in mid-summer. Focus on the deep hole at the next bend; keeping to the left and continuing to fish to the right. At this point (38.274679,-78.335558), you are 0.75 miles away from your vehicle and should think about fishing your way back upstream to take advantage of the deep pools you fished on the way down. However, if you have the energy, it's worth walking around the next corner to fish the curved section as well as the outflow where the river straightens again.

This view upstream to the bridge provides a perspective on the deep water. On a sunny weekend, this will be full of swimmers and people fishing from the bank.

The first riffle is 100 yards downstream from the bridge.

The water deepens beyond the riffle and the bottom structure is generally good.

The river takes a major turn and runs shallow around the bend.

Coming out of the major turn, fish against the right bank down to the tree in the distance.

Beyond the turnaround point, the river reverts to a sandy bottom.

Bottom Line

This is one of the better places to fish upstream from Elys Ford. Choose to go upstream if you are short on time.

Wolftown Road (Route 230)

Google Map Coordinates: 38.353032,-78.373976

Summary Rating

Parking	Red	Spin Fishing	Green
Canoe/Kayak Launch	Red	Fly Fishing	Green
Distance to River	Yellow	Trout	Red
Can Bike to River	Red	Smallmouth Bass	Red
Physical Fitness	Yellow	Pressure	Green
Scenery	Green	Overall	Red

If you are a glutton for punishment, fish here. This location is totally lacking as a fishing destination. It is far enough below the mountains that trout will not survive and the water runs so shallow that I do not believe smallmouth find this area attractive either. I have to admit that I only fished here once so my perspective may be skewed.

Special Regulations

There are no special fishing regulations in effect at this location.

Getting to the Stream

From US 29, turn west onto VA 230 and follow it to the bridge over the river. Park on the west side of the river at 38.35387, -78.37584.

You have two basic choices for parking. You can continue west to make a right turn onto VA 692 and park alongside the road. Alternatively, make a U-turn and tuck your vehicle into the VDOT easement pointing east. There is a metal traffic rail that extends most of the distance on the westbound side of the road that limits your ability to park on that side.

Canoe/Kayak comment: It is difficult to launch a boat at this location. While it's not hard to reach the river if you approach from the west on the left-hand side of the road, there is a large cattle guard underneath the bridge that blocks the downstream river. You will have to lift your boat over the guard to drop it into the shallow water on the downstream side. Unless the water is running high, you will end up having to walk downstream, pushing your boat, until the river narrows and picks up enough volume to float.

Environment and Fish

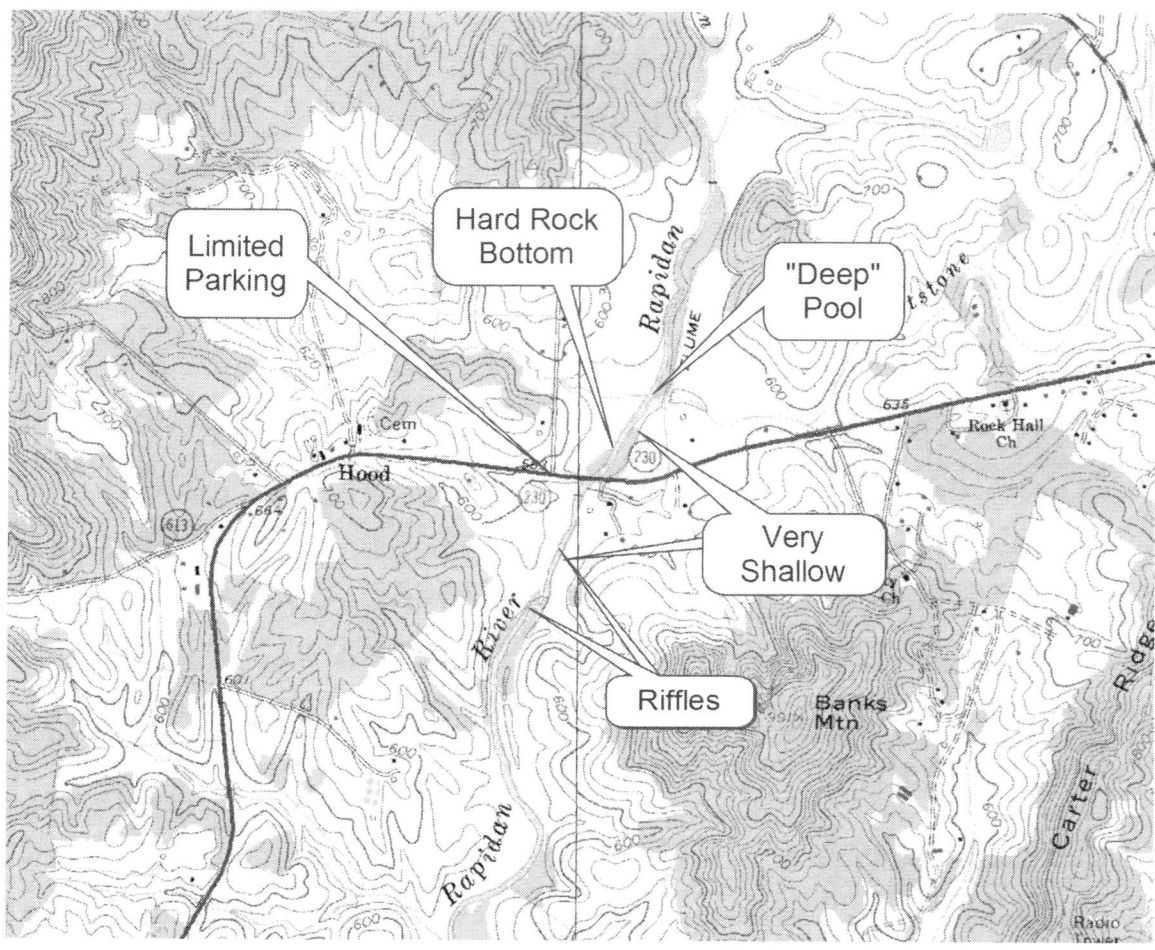

If you routinely drive up to the Blue Ridge, you may take VA 230 as a shortcut and wonder about the Rapidan as you take a quick look while darting across the bridge. The more curious may have actually stopped and walked over to stare at the pool underneath the bridge. If you do this at the right time, your adrenaline will pump as you see a cluster of fish holding in the cool water. Don't get all fired up. This is one of the worst places on the Rapidan to fish. There is absolutely nothing redeeming about this location. And those fish? They are all fallfish. As I did my research for this book, I did not encounter any smallmouth bass or trout. **This is a really, really bad spot. Really!!**

Not only is the water "skinny", but the species of fish that inhabit this location are primarily fallfish and sunfish. In addition, if there was a gray area in terms of streambed access, this location, along with the next one immediately upriver, are the two places you should avoid. That said, canoe and kayak enthusiasts use this and the next point upstream to start/end floats; proving that this location is well used for recreational purposes. In fact, American Whitewater regards this location as the alternate take-out for the exciting whitewater run that begins in the Park during the Spring floods. The VDOT easement is exceptionally wide and extends an abnormal distance upstream of the bridge on the west side. All that said, I still recommend you stay away from this place.

Upstream

There is no cattle guard blocking access to the upstream stretch from the bridge. If you fished downstream first, you'll be startled at the dramatic difference in the streambed above the bridge. While downstream was a mix of small to medium sized rocks, the upstream bed appears to have been scoured clean – it's all flat rock. The first fishable structure is a set of parallel ridges 25 yards north of the bridge in the middle of the river that create a 3 foot deep cut holding fallfish. Beyond that spot, the river shallows until you reach the bend upriver where there is a 5 foot deep section near the turn. Walk on the right bank and fish towards the left since the deep section continues up around the next bend. There is a small stream coming in from the right at 38.35628,-78.371723 that creates another deep spot. At that point, you are a little over one third of a mile from the bridge. What lays in front of you is a wide, shallow expanse of river that is not worth further investigation.

There is a cattle guard strung underneath the bridge that presents a significant obstacle to kayakers.

The initial look upstream at 362 cfs is encouraging. It looks like nice trout water. Very deceptive.

The river continues to shallow with random deep pools at the bends.

This spot has a vibrant population of fallfish.

The farther upstream you go, the shallower it gets.

Eventually, the river breaks out of the narrow twists and turns to run, inches deep, into the distance.

Downstream

The best way to get to the river is to approach from the west on the north side of the road. Once you climb down the boulders that support the bridge, you need to squeeze through the heavy metal cattle guard suspended from the bridge. What lays in front is a promising looking stretch of shallow, rocky streambed. It is made up of small to medium sized rocks with a boulder or two mixed in for diversity. Early in the year, at 370 cfs, the water coursing across this section is about 18 inches deep. At summer lows, it will slow to a dribble and force you to look for the cuts and pools. The deeper area is on the right-hand bank as you move downstream. There are some large fallfish that live near the brush that lines the bank, but no smallmouth. If you float poppers or large dry flies, there will be a fight between the fallfish and sunfish as to who will eat first. After the first hundred yards, the river shallows until it runs down a small drop in elevation to form a pool at the base (38.351964,-78.375403). Farther downstream at

38.35018, -78.37642, the river tightens as it takes a quick jog to the left and drops over a rock ledge into a deeper hole where there is another ledge running parallel to the shore. It gets deep on the left-hand bank; forcing you to the right to move farther downstream. A small feeder stream joins the river from the right that might hold trout in its upper elevations, but it is clearly on private property and you should not investigate. The river pools up to several feet in depth at this point. A walk farther downstream confirms that the river shallows again and the only thing that would be produced by further progress is sweat.

The first fishable water below the cattle guard is on the other side of the riffles.

The left bank holds a dense population of fallfish.

The river is inches deep as flows into the valley.

This is the only deep spot downstream.

Bottom Line

I cannot be more emphatic regarding my opinion on this access point. It is simply not worth the gas or the energy to fish. There is nothing here worth your time. No smallmouth, no trout.

Graves Mill (Route 662)

Google Map Coordinates: 38.370143,-78.364642

Summary Rating

Parking	Red	Spin Fishing	Green
Canoe/Kayak Launch	Red	Fly Fishing	Yellow
Distance to River	Yellow	Trout	Red
Can Bike to River	Red	Smallmouth Bass	Red
Physical Fitness	Red	Pressure	Green
Scenery	Green	Overall	Red

Like the Wolftown road access point, there is nothing worthwhile about this spot; no positive comments. I believe this is in the dead zone between the start of both the upstream trout fishing and the downstream smallmouth fishing. Simply put, don't bother stopping here.

Special Regulations

There are no special fishing regulations in effect at this location.

Getting to the Stream

From US 29, turn west onto VA 231. Bear right at VA 662 and follow it to the bridge. Park on the west side of the bridge.

There is a dirt road that goes to the river from the north side of the road once you cross the bridge. I know this is considered an informal parking area and put-in for kayakers. However, it is on private property and I recommend you stay within the VDOT easement at the edge of the road.

Canoe/Kayak comment: Most people use the beaten dirt road on the north side of the bridge to reach the river. I do not recommend using that approach since it crosses private property. The alternative is to drop your boat down the steep bank next to the bridge. That could make for some tough maneuvering to reach the water. Once in the water, it is extremely shallow downstream of the bridge and, at lower water levels, your trip will start with a hike instead of a float.

Environment and Fish

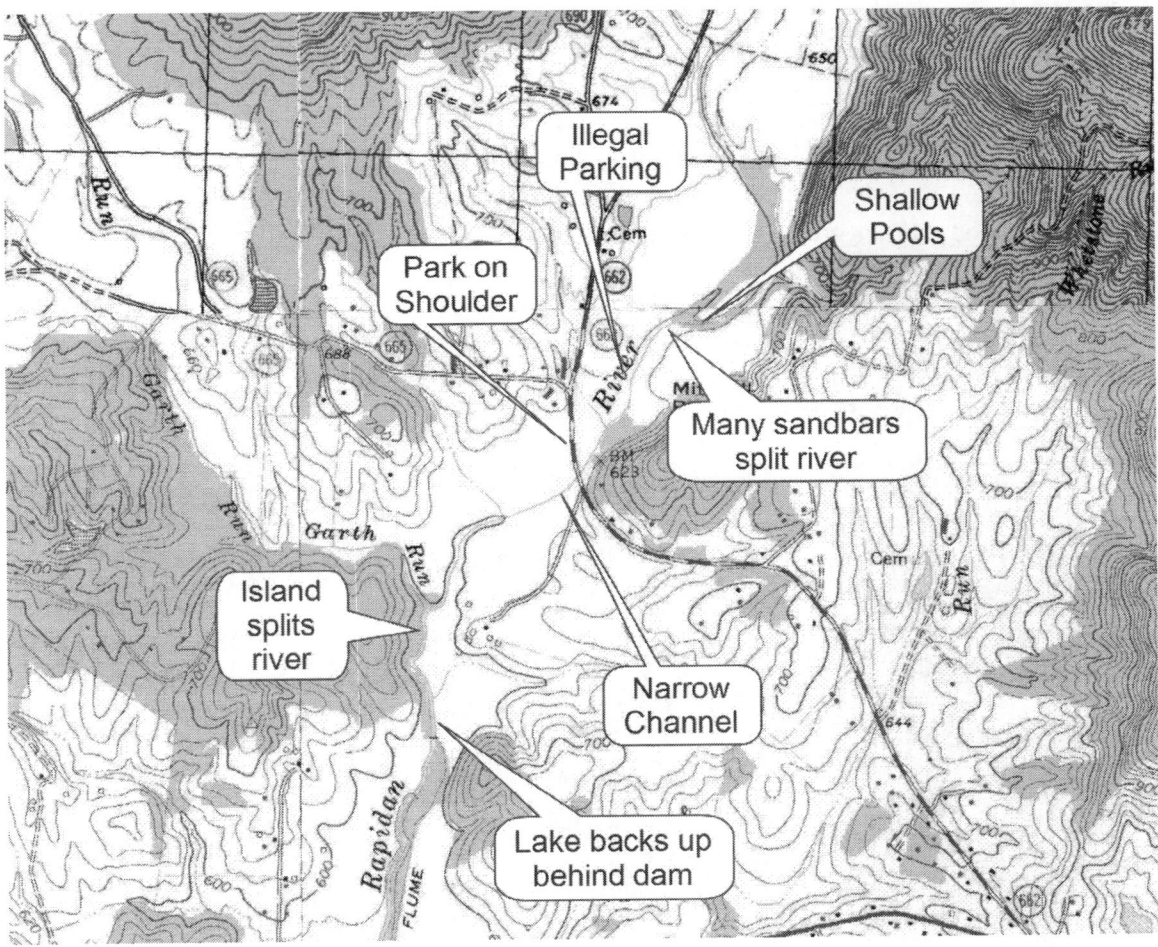

My opinion on this section of the Rapidan is identical to what you just read regarding the Wolftown Road access. While you might be optimistic since this bridge crossing is closer to the National Park, I confirmed with the VDGIF that the river upstream is usually "trout free." They cautioned that the downstream boundary of trout habitat depends on weather and water temperature; adding that, in normal times, they rarely see trout farther than a mile south of the Park. This access point is a good distance beyond that threshold.

Like the Wolftown Road access point, this is a gray area. There are no cautioning signs restricting access and it is used by kayakers as a put-in and take-out point demonstrating that it meets at least the minimum navigability standards associated with recreational use. But since there is no compelling reason to fish here, you should not. The water is skinny and only provides a home to fallfish and sunfish.

As I did my research for this book, I did not encounter any smallmouth bass or trout. **This is a really, really bad spot.**

Upstream

If you point your rod upstream, you will get an initial adrenaline rush based on the look and feel of the water. It appears to be perfect trout habitat with one key issue -- temperature. It's too hot for trout survival this far from the Blue Ridge. Just like downstream, the only fish living here are fallfish and sunfish. In general, the river adopts a mountain character as you move upstream. It's narrow and uniformly rocky with the minimum amount of sand covering the streambed. Even though it is in a river valley, it winds back and forth with some velocity across gradient breaks at regular intervals. Each bend in the river produces a deep area where you can catch as many sunfish and fallfish as you care to pull in. Since these fish are not interesting to either me or, I presume, you, I will skip further commentary on the river upstream - it's not worth either the words or the paper to provide a more detailed description.

The view downstream to the bridge at 512 cfs is encouraging and offers false hope of a nice spot.

The area to the left is the canoe put-in that is at the end of the dirt road leading to the river.

The fallfish and sunfish enjoy the hiding places offered by the collective structure at the bends.

A different view at 309 cfs shows how the water level has dropped by summer.

Each drop in elevation terminates in a pool that is populated with sunfish or fallfish.

On a sunny day, this looks idyllic, but not if you want to catch bass or trout.

Downstream

The best way to get to the river is to use the easement on the downstream side from the east. It's a shame this water will not support trout because what lays in front of you is good-looking trout water. There is a long rock ridge that stretches down the middle of the river terminating in a pool underneath an overhanging bush on the left bank. If it were actually worthwhile fish here, that would be where you would direct your attention. Work your way down the right-hand bank and fish left until you reach a bend in the river. That's the start of an extended pool that holds large fallfish. The deep section continues on the right-hand bank until you approach a downstream run where the river shallows out.

Continue downstream to the junction of Garth Run with the Rapidan (38.367056,-78.370521). While Garth Run does have trout in its upper reaches, this part of Garth Run it is on private property and is off-limits. Downstream of the junction, the river briefly deepens and then continues to wind its way around small islands and rocky ridges where it remains shallow with a few randomly dispersed deep pools until it reaches 38.36571,-78.370478. This is the head of a 150 foot island that splits the river in two.

Both channels are narrow with the right-hand side being the more scenic of the two; having a nice rock cliff face at the downstream end. At the base of the split, the two channels rejoin to form a deep pool. This is the start of a "lake" section backed up by the low dam at 38.362884,-78.369974. Stay on the right-hand bank and fish left. At that point, you are approximately 3/4 of a mile from the bridge and are probably wishing you had followed my advice not to fish here. Given the great water in the Park a few minutes upstream of the bridge crossing, why waste energy in a location that you know is going to be bad?

If you are foolish enough to spend time here, the easiest place to get to the river is on the southeastern side of the bridge.

The bridge splits the river into two shallow channels.

If there were actually trout, you would start to become excited right here.

At high water levels in the spring, it is still easy to wade as long as you stick close to the banks.

This is the rock cliff mentioned above.

And it all eventually spins out into a wide, deep lake that leads up to a low water dam and adds up to a colossal waste of time.

Bottom Line

Again, I need to be emphatic in my strong recommendation that you never lay eyes on the river in this section. It's not worth the gas, it's not worth the energy. If you have come this far, keep going because the trout water is only a few minutes farther north.

Rapidan Trout Overview

This extract from the VDGIF map of the Rapidan Wildlife Management Area (WMA) indicates the specific locations that I will discuss in subsequent chapters. We all should be grateful for the efforts that led to the creation of the WMA since it fills in the gaps along the river created by the erratic boundary of the Shenandoah National Park.

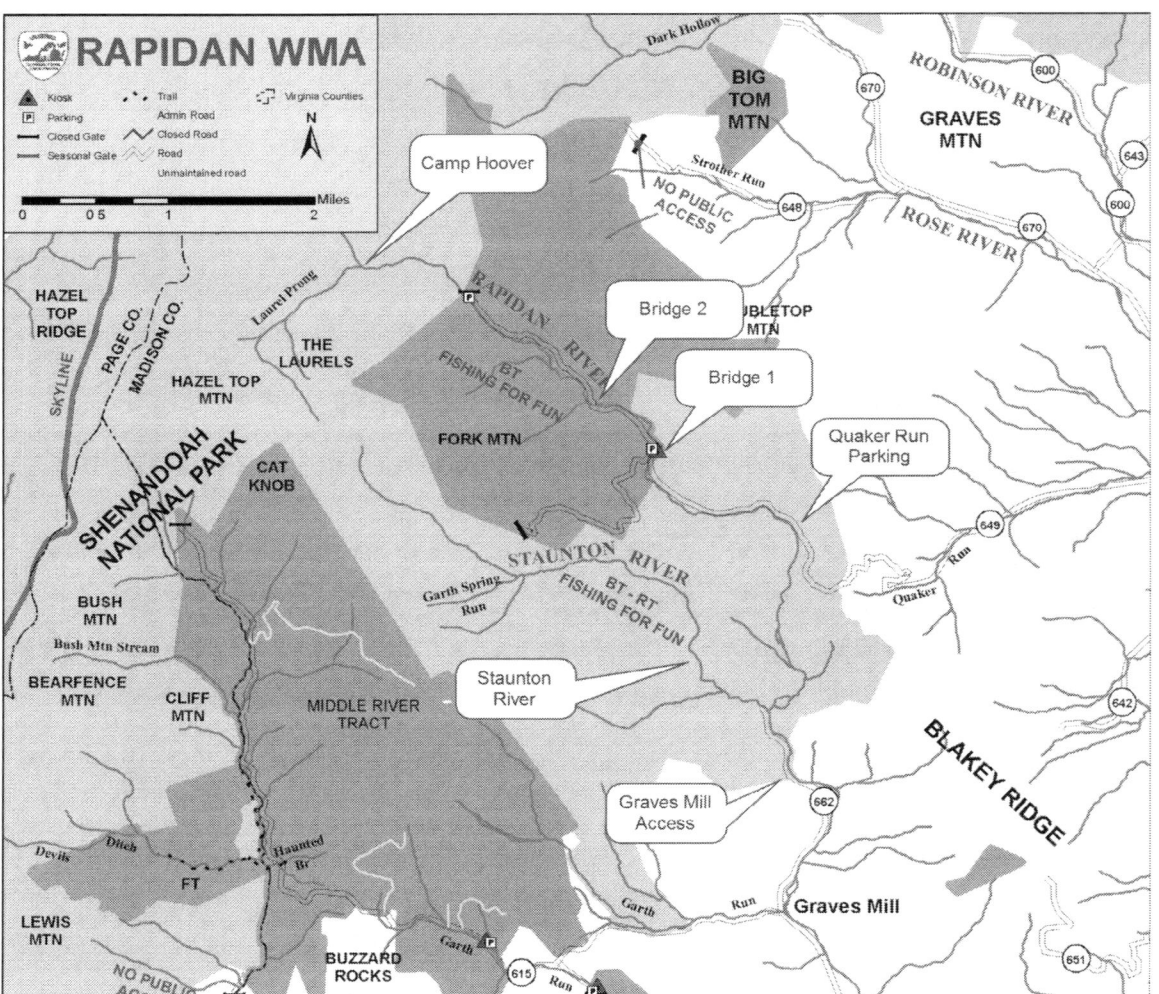

Underlying map provided by the Virginia Department of Game and Inland Fisheries and used with permission

Hatch Chart

I need to provide a caveat with the hatch chart below. This reflects my experience and shows the flies I typically use when fishing the Blue Ridge. When I did some checking against other hatch charts available on the Internet, it looks like it is consistent with most other recommendations. However, use it as a guide and take flies in various sizes to match what you actually encounter on the stream.

Fly Name	Jan	Feb	Mar	Apr	May	Jun	Jul	Aug	Sep	Oct	Nov	Dec	Size
Brown Elk Hair Caddis			■	■									14 - 16
Black Elk Hair Caddis			■	■									14 - 18
Blue Quill				■									16 - 18
Quill Gordon			■	■									12 - 16
Black Gnat				■	■								16 - 18
Hendrickson				■	■								14 - 16
March Brown					■								10 - 14
Sulphur					■	■							14 - 18
Black Stonefly					■	■							8 - 10
Yellow Sally						■							12 - 14
Light Cahill						■							14 - 16
Mosquito						■	■	■	■				12 - 18
Cricket							■	■	■				8 - 14
Hopper						■	■	■	■				10 - 14
Ant					■	■	■	■	■				14 - 18
Beetles				■	■	■	■	■	■				12 - 16
Attractors				■	■	■	■	■	■	■			14 - 18
Mr. Rapidan			■	■	■	■	■	■	■	■			8 - 14
Adams	■	■	■	■	■	■			■	■	■	■	12 - 16
Blue Wing Olive	■	■	■	■	■	■					■	■	16 - 20

If this seems confusing, just load up with Murray's Mr. Rapidan, Adams, mosquitoes and some hares ear nymphs.

If you use spin gear, take small gold or silver spinners (like Panther Martins) and you will do just fine.

Graves Mill (Shenandoah National Park)

Google Map Coordinates: 38.436917,-78.367002

Summary Rating

Parking	Green	Spin Fishing	Green
Canoe/Kayak Launch	Green	Fly Fishing	Green
Distance to River	Green	Trout	Green
Can Bike to River	Red	Smallmouth Bass	Red
Physical Fitness	Red	Pressure	Red
Scenery	Green	Overall	Yellow

This is one of the most heavily fished parts of the Rapidan River. It is the start of trout water. It is also the last logical place to launch a boat.

Special Regulations

"Only single-point hook artificial lures may be used-no bait. On those streams open to harvest, the creel limit is 6 trout per day with a 9-inch minimum size for brook trout and a 7-inch minimum size for brown and rainbow trout. On all other streams open to fishing, catch and release regulations apply. The release of any brown trout back into any Park stream is prohibited and brown trout less than 7 inches must be disposed of within the Park but away from Park streams, roads or trails. This is an effort to limit the impacts of brown trout on the native brook trout populations. Contact the Shenandoah National Park at 540-999-3500 for the annual list of streams open to harvest." - VDGIF

The Rapidan is not on the list of streams open to harvest. It is strictly catch and release.

Getting to the Stream

From US 29, turn west at the Sheetz station on VA 230. Follow VA 230 (and the signs to Graves Mill) veering onto VA 662 (Graves Mill Road). Stay on VA 662 and take a right on Graves Road. The turn may not be obvious if you are moving at speed, be alert. Follow Graves Road to the end and park.

The trail leaves the parking area at the north end of the lot and parallels the left-hand side of the river for several miles all the way up to the Quaker Run turnoff described in a subsequent chapter.

Canoe/Kayak comment: This is the last place on the Rapidan that American Whitewater documents as a put-in location. As you move farther upstream into the park, the water becomes tighter and rougher.

Environment and Fish

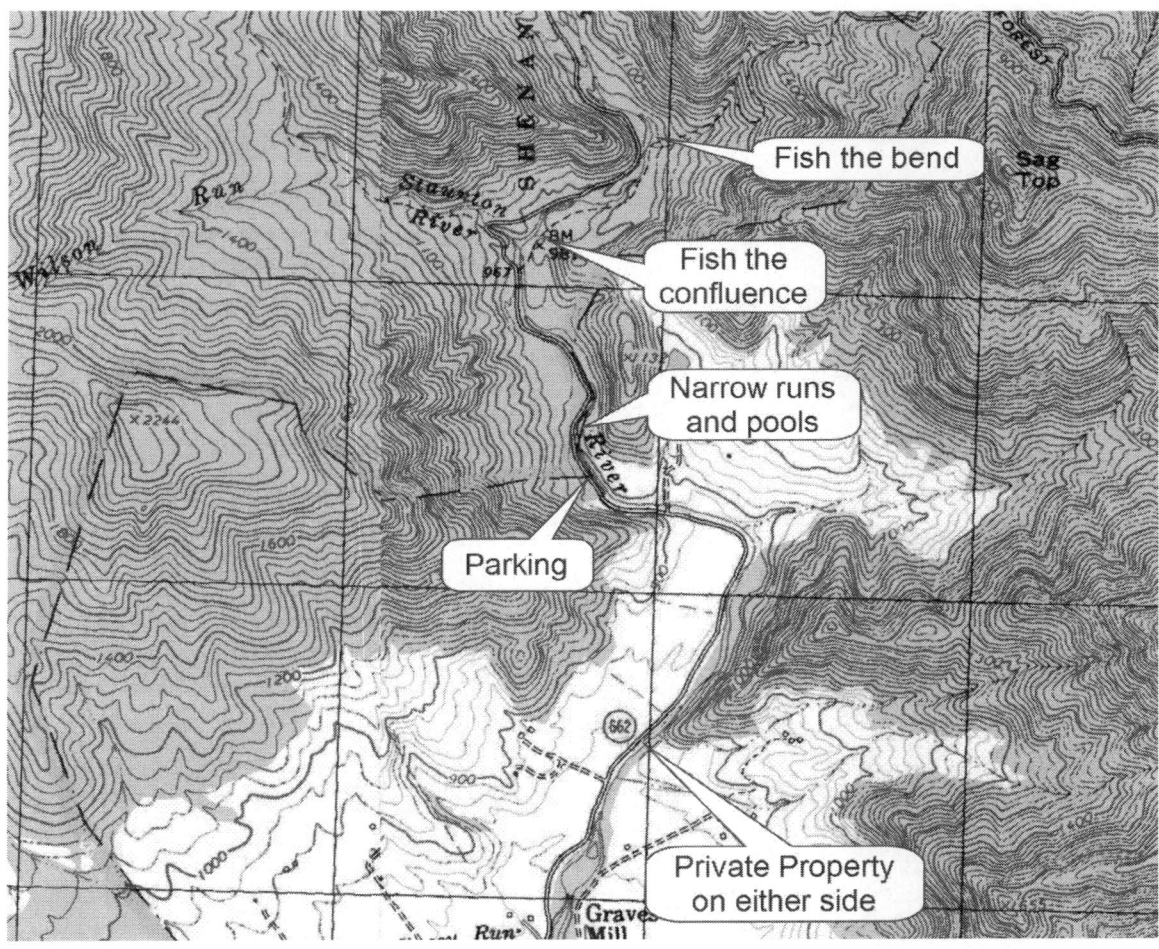

This chapter covers the section of the Rapidan between the National Park boundary and the confluence with the Staunton River. Out of all the Rapidan's trout water, this section is the most heavily fished. It's easily accessible, has a good road leading into it, plenty of parking and a wide, smooth trail with numerous beaten paths leading to the river. Therefore, it doesn't pay to walk anywhere to distance yourself from perceived pressure. You may as well hang a right once inside the Park boundary and make your way to the river.

Even though this is heavily fished, it does not mean that it is uniformly accessible. In places, dense brush forms a thick barrier between the main trail and the river bank. You have to twist and turn between saplings and bushes to make it to the river if you choose not to use one of the many beaten fisherman's paths that lead from the main trail. While they are not marked with official park service signs, the crushed leaves and packed dirt provide ample indication of where to go. I guess this is the appropriate place to provide a warning. If you are going to bushwhack anywhere in the upper Rapidan, do not bother to assemble your rod. The trees are tight, the bushes are thick and you will become frustrated as you try and poke a long rod into tight places. Be patient and wait until you get to the edge of the stream to assemble your gear.

Once you reach the river, the banks are low, easy to negotiate and you can hop down into a streambed that has the characteristic mountain mix of boulders and rocks. The sand that plagued you in the bass water farther south is gone forever. Since this is the section below the confluence with the Staunton, there is usually plenty of flow. The trade-off is that this is the lower extremity of cold water and, depending on the weather, you may or may not find trout the farther you move downstream from the confluence. In fact, I talked to one of the VDGIF biologists and he told me that this is a transition zone between trout and smallmouth bass. In a good year, trout may be found a mile south of the Park boundary but, given the issues associated with accessing that part of the river, you are stuck fishing from the parking lot upstream.

None of that should keep you from enjoying this section of the river. Every large rock formation marks a pool that is at least a few feet deep. In fact, the streambed is tight and the rocks are large. At the corners, this forces the ample volume of water into compressed spaces adding velocity that makes it difficult to fish effectively. The pools are large enough to fish with spin gear, but the best weapon you can use here is a fly rod.

When you first encounter the river, it will flow wide and shallow over a staircase of gradient breaks. If you can find small sections of calm water, they are worth fishing - even if the spot is a 1 foot section behind a boulder. Work your way quickly upstream from calm section to calm section. When the vegetation is thick and water fast, you'll find yourself restricted to the edge of the stream and walking in the shallows. The eastern bank is steep and sandy and you do not gain anything by crawling up the bank and walking along the river. If you do that, not only will you have to fight your way through the thick vegetation, picking up plenty of ticks along the way, but you also face the challenge of sliding back down to river level; making enough noise to scare the skittish trout. Finally, the east bank is not in the Park and is on private property. By itself, that's a reason to stay away from it.

If you can deal with the crowds, the first 200 feet of the river upstream from the parking lot is a good place to warm up. At 38.438556,-78.367388, the river takes a sharp turn to the east with the next 75 feet being tight and rocky. Move to the left-hand bank; skipping the shallow unproductive water, and start fishing again at the broad pool at the head of the rapids. Fish up and around the corner to encounter a broad rocky island on the right that stretches another 50 feet upstream. Depending on the water levels, it may or may not be useful to fish this portion of the river. The good news is that the next 150 feet is usually good. The river broadens and, although it can be shallow at times, it provides good habitat and holding areas.

This continues up to where the river turns sharply west at 38.441107,-78.367656. At this point, both banks are in the Park and you do not need to be concerned about trespassing if you step on the right-hand bank. After taking a sharp pitch downward, creating fast water at the bend, there is another good 75 foot stretch that leads into the next turn to the north. The river breaks up into small channels with another rocky island on the right-hand side (38.442476,-78.369577) and takes a final turn to the north leading into the confluence with the Staunton. Again, the good stretch is beyond the rocky island with the area immediately downstream of the confluence being my personal favorite in this section of the Rapidan.

Look for small, beaten trails leading towards the river from the main path.

Finally! Good trout water after doing all the bass fishing from the confluence all the way up through the horrible water at Wolftown Road and the Route 622 bridge.

This is classic Shenandoah trout water. In addition to the larger pools, target fish in the small bits of slack water above and below the major rock structure.

The river staircases with shallow runs terminating in riffles.

Wherever you find a major conglomeration of large rocks like this, there will be a deep pool that holds the larger fish.

Fish the area below the confluence with the Staunton River.

Bottom Line

Every trout section of the Rapidan has merits. The only disadvantage of this spot is its closeness to the parking area and associated pressure. It may experience the greatest mortality and have the lowest density of fish since the fish are caught several times during their life. I have not verified that with the VDGIF -- just my opinion.

Staunton River

Google Map Coordinates: 38.443993,-78.36947

Summary Rating

Parking	Green	Spin Fishing	Red
Canoe/Kayak Launch	Red	Fly Fishing	Red
Distance to River	Red	Trout	Green
Can Bike to River	Red	Smallmouth Bass	Red
Physical Fitness	Red	Pressure	Green
Scenery	Green	Overall	Green

The Staunton River is a key tributary into the Rapidan. It is also one of the jewels of the Shenandoah National Park since it is tricky and technical to fish while being within a reasonable hike from the parking area. The difficulty, combined with the hike, conspires to filter most of the pressure. If you see anybody, it will probably be a hiker. Since the stream pitches back and forth frequently, even if there were another angler on the water, you probably would not see him. This area is rated as Red for both spin and fly anglers as a result of the tight, tight narrow course of the river and the respectable amount of overhanging vegetation.

Special Regulations

"Only single-point hook artificial lures may be used-no bait. On those streams open to harvest, the creel limit is 6 trout per day with a 9-inch minimum size for brook trout and a 7-inch minimum size for brown and rainbow trout. On all other streams open to fishing, catch and release regulations apply. The release of any brown trout back into any Park stream is prohibited and brown trout less than 7 inches must be disposed of within the Park but away from Park streams, roads or trails. This is an effort to limit the impacts of brown trout on the native brook trout populations. Contact the Shenandoah National Park at 540-999-3500 for the annual list of streams open to harvest." - VDGIF

The Rapidan is not on the list of streams open to harvest. It is strictly catch and release.

Getting to the Stream

From US 29, turn west at the Sheetz station on VA 230. Follow VA 230 (and the signs to Graves Mill) veering onto VA 662 (Graves Mill Road). Stay on VA 662 and take a right on Graves Road. The turn may not be obvious if you are moving at speed, be alert. Follow Graves Road to the end and park.

Follow the trail north along the river. The Staunton River intersects the trail approximately a half mile from the parking area. It is impossible to miss the junction since it is marked with a tall concrete pillar at a very obvious fork in the trail.

Canoe/Kayak comment: I have never heard of anyone hauling a boat a mile upstream to drop it into the Staunton.

Environment and Fish

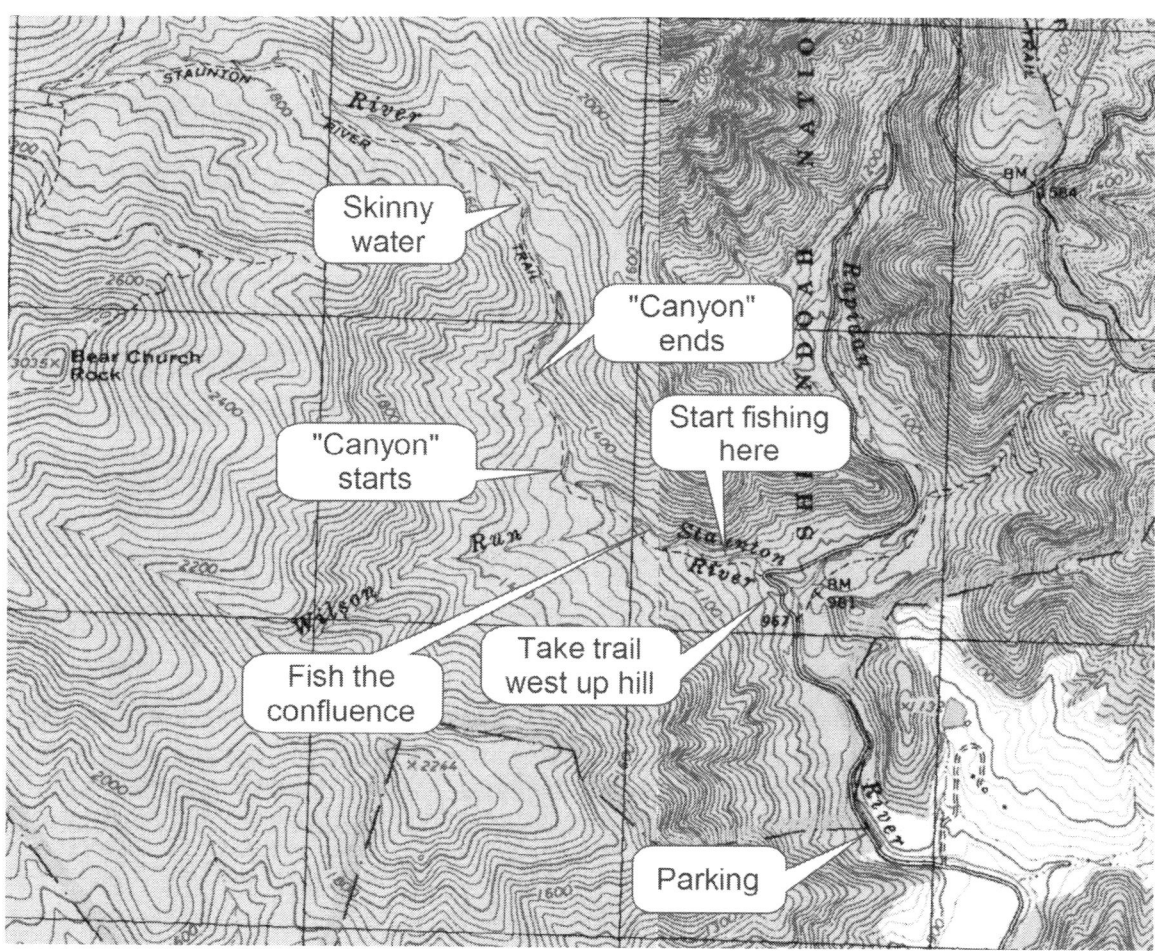

From the junction, the trail pitches up and forces you to climb a moderate grade. Approximately a quarter mile later, you find yourself standing at the edge of the river. This is not the place to begin fishing. The water runs over a wide, slick rock face that is dangerous to traverse. Instead, walk another 25 yards up the trail and beat your way through the underbrush to get to the river above the smooth pitch. I will give this advice once more. Do not assemble your rod until you are at the edge of the stream. The brush is thick, tight and, if you have a long rod, you will find yourself spending more time pulling it out of trees and potentially snapping your line or, even worse, your rod tip as you stagger to the water. See the gear chapter for suggestions on what to carry as a backup rod.

Unfortunately, or perhaps fortunately, there are no beaten paths to the river from the trail as there are on the main stem of the Rapidan. I believe this is a good thing. It protects the river from all but the most adventurous. You need to be in decent physical condition and willing to clamber over tall boulders or scoot under and through tight places to fish this river. The thick underbrush provides a protective barrier to keep the faint of heart at bay.

After you wipe the sweat off your brow and catch your breath, you will be taken aback by the simple beauty of this tight stream. Ideally, you reached the stream early in the morning when you can enjoy the rising sun punching through the overhanging trees; creating a spectacular bright green glow as it filters through the leaves. While the Rapidan below the confluence was typically 20-30 feet across, the Staunton is lucky to reach 10. Assuming you avoided the rainy season, the water in front of you will run steady and calm. During the intense Spring runoff or in the Fall rainy season, there will be more water here than you can deal with. When there's a lot of water, there's not much room and it becomes unfishable. In fact, when the water is high, it is dangerous. The best time to fish this section is in the late Spring or early Fall prior to the spawn.

In terms of structure, it is all generally the same. The water streams between large boulders following tight cuts that dump into "deep" pools. Even though the larger pools have decent depth and can be up to 3 feet deep, the water moves quickly. When combined with the tight, overhanging vegetation, this is where you need to deploy your "short game." Whether fishing with spin or fly gear, use a short stick. The only exception is for those who have adapted to Tenkara fly fishing. Even using a Tenkara rod, you will find yourself collapsing several of the sections into the handle to shorten it when you need to pop the fly into a tight spot. A long cast on the Staunton is 15 feet. There is just not that much room to maneuver.

Beyond casting, physical movement from place to place is restricted. There is no trail at the edge of the river. You are in the water, standing on rocks and climbing over boulders to move upriver. This ends up being a good thing since it positions you downstream of each pool. If you approach carefully, the downstream boulders will shield most of your body from the wary trout that cling to the bottom of the upstream pool. You only get one shot at presentation – so get into position and be careful on that first cast. If using fly gear, avoid false casting. The pictures below tell the rest of the story regarding the rough terrain.

There are two terrain features that deserve comment. The first is where a small feeder stream joins the river from the south at approximately 38.44603, -78.37528. This creates a more robust, fishable section in the area immediately downstream before the river heaves over a sharp drop and spreads back out.

The other is the "gorge" that exists between 38.44694,-78.37692 and 38.44795,-78.37831. Up until the point in time you enter the gorge, you have relatively uncomplicated access back to the main trail. Once in, you have to gut it out for at least 400 feet before being able to climb easily back to the trail.

The trail that parallels the river is broad and level. Unfortunately, you cannot use a bike on any of the trails in the Shenandoah National Park near the Rapidan.

This concrete post marks the turn to the Staunton. Take a left and walk up the hill.

If you enter the river as described above, this is your first look at the water.

You do not have to walk far to find your first pool.

The river is peppered with pools that look just like this. The challenge is the tightly wrapped vegetation that hangs low over the river; presenting a fly fisherman's obstacle course.

There is a significant amount of elevation gain associated with fishing this river. Be prepared to climb up some rock walls to get to the next set of pools.

Hide behind the downstream boulders.

Spots like this make it worth the walk.

Bottom Line

The Staunton River is a Shenandoah National Park treasure. Since it is difficult to fish and requires a hike of three quarters of a mile just to start, it does not experience significant pressure. This is not a river for beginners -- regardless of whether you are a spin angler or a fly rodder. Even spin fishermen must have mastered the short, accurate cast on ultralight gear or gird themselves to experience a day of total frustration.

Upper Rapidan (Quaker Run)

Google Map Coordinates: 38.46257,-78.365602

Summary Rating

Parking	Yellow	Spin Fishing	Green
Canoe/Kayak Launch	Green	Fly Fishing	Green
Distance to River	Green	Trout	Green
Can Bike to River	Red	Smallmouth Bass	Red
Physical Fitness	Red	Pressure	Red
Scenery	Green	Overall	Yellow

The popularity of this section of the Rapidan is what produces the overall rating of yellow. The farther you are willing to walk downstream from the parking area, the greener the overall rating becomes.

Special Regulations

"Only single-point hook artificial lures may be used-no bait. On those streams open to harvest, the creel limit is 6 trout per day with a 9-inch minimum size for brook trout and a 7-inch minimum size for brown and rainbow trout. On all other streams open to fishing, catch and release regulations apply. The release of any brown trout back into any Park stream is prohibited and brown trout less than 7 inches must be disposed of within the Park but away from Park streams, roads or trails. This is an effort to limit the impacts of brown trout on the native brook trout populations. Contact the Shenandoah National Park at 540-999-3500 for the annual list of streams open to harvest." - VDGIF

The Rapidan is not on the list of streams open to harvest. It is strictly catch and release.

Getting to the Stream

North: From US 29 continue south past Culpeper. Turn Right at Hoover Road (VA 609) and follow it towards Syria. Turn right at North Blue Ridge Turnpike (VA 231) to go north, continuing towards Syria. Take the first left onto Old Blue Ridge Turnpike (VA 670) at a "Y" in the road near an old grocery. Follow VA 670 for a little over 4 miles to Quaker Run Road. Turn left onto Quaker Run and follow it to the river.

South: From US 29, turn left onto South Main Street at Madison. Make a slight left onto North Blue Ridge Turnpike (VA 231) to go north, continuing towards Syria. Take the first left onto Old Blue Ridge

Turnpike (VA 670) at a "Y" in the road near an old grocery. Follow VA 670 for a little over 4 miles to Quaker Run Road. Turn left onto Quaker Run and follow it to the river.

There is a wide parking area where the road intersects the river at 38.46257,-78.365602.

Canoe/Kayak comment: I have never heard of anyone putting a boat into the river at this location. I suppose you could, but I don't recommend it since there are numerous blowdowns across the river that are dangerous if you were to charge into them when the water is high enough to make it a feasible run.

Environment and Fish

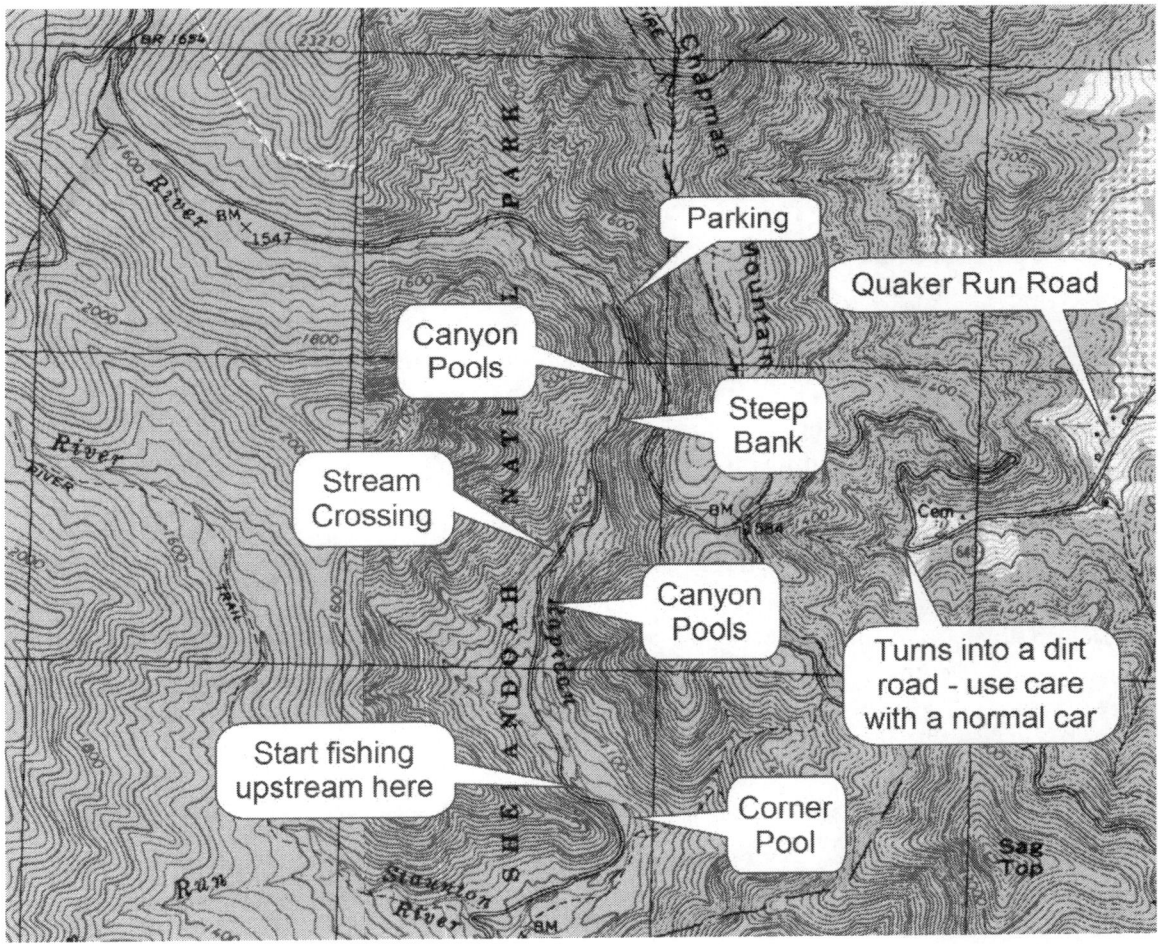

There are two distinct sections at Quaker Run and both deserve your consideration. The only question you have to answer is, "How far do you want to walk?" After bumping over the rough road from Syria, you're probably anxious to fish and will instantly see the spectacular pool at the base of the small parking lot -- just like 100 other anglers. Therefore, your choice is simple. Begin to fish immediately or follow the trail from the parking lot a half mile south until it crosses the river (38.455227,-78.367437). At that point, either fish your way back up to your car or to continue on the easy path that parallels the river all the way to Graves Mill. There is a difference.

Downstream from the crossing

Well, I have to admit I lied a little bit. If you start fishing immediately downstream of the crossing, your day will be a pure nightmare given the difficulty in working down a steep drop-off into a narrow gorge that creates numerous sheer plunge pools protected by gigantic boulders. It's much less dangerous to fish heading upstream. Given that, keep walking on the path for another 0.6 miles. You will start to get anxious -- especially if it's been a long drive -- as you listen to the roar of the river on the left. Depending on the amount of vegetation, the trail will edge next to the river approximately 0.3 miles from the crossing at 38.45304, -78.36831. That is the start of the extremely physical stretch that I describe later. Stay on the trail for the full distance until the river pops up on the left near 38.44786,-78.36589. At that point, the river angles off to the left to move around the corner.

Follow the trail south another 25 yards and cut left through the brush to beat your way to the corner. There is a good pool there that you need to fish. Do not ignore the 25 yard flat run that spills out of it. Once you hit those two spots, fish your way back up the river. Initially, it will be fairly gentle, flowing without urgency since it runs flat with a slight downward pitch to move the water towards Graves Mill. For the next quarter mile, the water tumbles across medium sized rocks and boulders to create 1 to 2 foot plunge pools. The farther upstream you move, the tighter the river becomes and the more challenging it is to crawl over boulders that seem to grow larger and larger with every step.

The good news is that each of those large boulders creates a pool at its base. Some of the spots in this stretch are over 5 feet deep. Given that, you need to be careful where you step. This is not easy walking. You literally have to climb over boulders or slither under trees to move upstream. If you have the physical ability, your efforts will pay off handsomely since this section holds some of the larger trout. It is also the only decent section of the river for spin anglers to fish. In the upper reaches, the pools are wide enough to flip a small spinner and have enough runway for it to activate. That said, most of the upper Rapidan is fly fishing country and flies should be your weapon of choice.

Unlike the section immediately downstream of the parking lot, the trail remains fairly close to the river. As you crawl over and around the large boulders after the leaves are out and the brush fills in, you will assume that the trail is miles away. Although it's a difficult scramble up the bank most places, you can leave the river anywhere and get back on the trail. Therefore, if you run into an obstacle that you cannot negotiate, clamber back to the trail and walk around it.

This section of the Rapidan features pools large enough for spin fishermen to have a good day.

It also holds some amazing fish! Sorry for the bad picture, but I was anxious to get him back in the water.

Upon initially entering the river at the far turn, the river is shallow, but full of runs that twist their way around numerous rocks.

Continue walking up the river and carefully fish all of the wide spots. The water is deceptively clear and deep.

Eventually, the river begins to pick up elevation as it moves into the canyon.

As the banks become steep on either side, the width of the river compresses and the rocks seem to grow out of the streambed.

Finally, as the river enters the steepest pitch, movement is difficult and constrained severely by the sheer bank.

This scenic pool is at the top of the climb.

Upstream from the crossing

When compared to the downstream side of the crossing, upstream is dramatically easier. Downstream, the river narrows as it crashes into the sudden drop-off leading to the river valley far below. Upstream from the crossing, the river, while steep, courses through a gradually sloping canyon full of huge boulders that provide the key structural support for the innumerable deep pools.

Begin fishing at the crossing. You may assume that any pool so close to the main thoroughfare would be empty. Thankfully, there is a strong catch and release ethic in the Park that preserves the fish for the next guy. Hopefully, you subscribe to that approach as well. If you don't, please throw this book away right now.

The pool immediately upstream from the crossing is wide and deep -- a classic and representative example of what you will encounter as you move upstream. Once you start walking up the river, it captures you in a deep canyon that makes exit back to the road a tough climb. The depth of the canyon varies as you move up the river. There are a few logical exit points, but, in general, once in the canyon, you are in it until you get back to the parking lot. Frankly, you will not mind a bit.

Fair warning. Staying in the river may be as challenging as leaving. There is no trail next to the river and you must scramble up and around large boulders that get slick when wet. The spectacular pattern of pool -- drop -- pool keeps your interest and gives you plenty of water to fish. Given the proximity to the parking lot, you can expect to see other people as you move upstream. It is heavily fished and you may want to walk the extra distance to the downstream section that sees less pressure. I am continually amazed at how dramatically the pressure drops off the farther you walk from the car. I can give folks some slack since they can see the exciting plunge pools from the road and the siren song of great water with decent sized fish will pull all but the most hard-core to the river's edge quickly.

Don't ignore the pool immediately above the crossing.

It leads into several additional pools that are equally deep and productive as you walk up the river.

All are wide enough for spin fishermen to enjoy.

There is a steep drop in elevation between the parking lot and the crossing; confirmed by the dramatic plunges.

The trail leading to the crossing is at the right of the picture. Note the steepness of the bank.

Okay.... Go ahead and fish the pool by the parking lot – everyone does!

Bottom Line

I prefer the section downstream from the crossing to fishing upstream to the parking area. Either choice is good and both are worth the long drive over the bumpy mountain road. If the parking lot is full, fishing is equally spectacular farther upriver. Read on!

Upper Rapidan (1st Bridge)

Google Map Coordinates: 38.46257,-78.365602

Summary Rating

Parking	Red	Spin Fishing	Green
Canoe/Kayak Launch	Red	Fly Fishing	Green
Distance to River	Yellow	Trout	Green
Can Bike to River	Red	Smallmouth Bass	Red
Physical Fitness	Red	Pressure	Red
Scenery	Green	Overall	Yellow

While the area below the first bridge could be rated as Green, once you are beyond the bridge the pressure is intense as a result of the numerous campsites that speckle the edge of the river; forcing the overall rating to Yellow. Below the bridge, you must walk a short distance through the undergrowth to reach the river. Above the bridge, you can step from some campsites directly into the water.

Special Regulations

"Only single-point hook artificial lures may be used-no bait. On those streams open to harvest, the creel limit is 6 trout per day with a 9-inch minimum size for brook trout and a 7-inch minimum size for brown and rainbow trout. On all other streams open to fishing, catch and release regulations apply. The release of any brown trout back into any Park stream is prohibited and brown trout less than 7 inches must be disposed of within the Park but away from Park streams, roads or trails. This is an effort to limit the impacts of brown trout on the native brook trout populations. Contact the Shenandoah National Park at 540-999-3500 for the annual list of streams open to harvest." - VDGIF

The Rapidan is not on the list of streams open to harvest. It is strictly catch and release.

Getting to the Stream

North: From US 29 continue south past Culpeper. Turn Right at Hoover Road (VA 609) and follow it towards Syria. Turn right at North Blue Ridge Turnpike (VA 231) to go north, continuing towards Syria. Take the first left onto Old Blue Ridge Turnpike (VA 670) at a "Y" in the road near an old grocery. Follow VA 670 for a little over 4 miles to Quaker Run Road. Turn left onto Quaker Run and follow it to the river.

North: From US 29, turn left onto South Main Street at Madison. Make a slight left onto North Blue Ridge Turnpike (VA 231) to go north, continuing towards Syria. Take the first left onto Old Blue Ridge Turnpike (VA 670) at a "Y" in the road near an old grocery. Follow VA 670 for a little over 4 miles to Quaker Run Road. Turn left onto Quaker Run and follow it to the river.

The road will parallel the river. In addition to the numerous turnoffs on the left, there is a large parking area south of the first bridge on the left at 38.46995,-78.38356.

Canoe/Kayak comment: Not applicable. This is outside of the normal range.

Environment and Fish

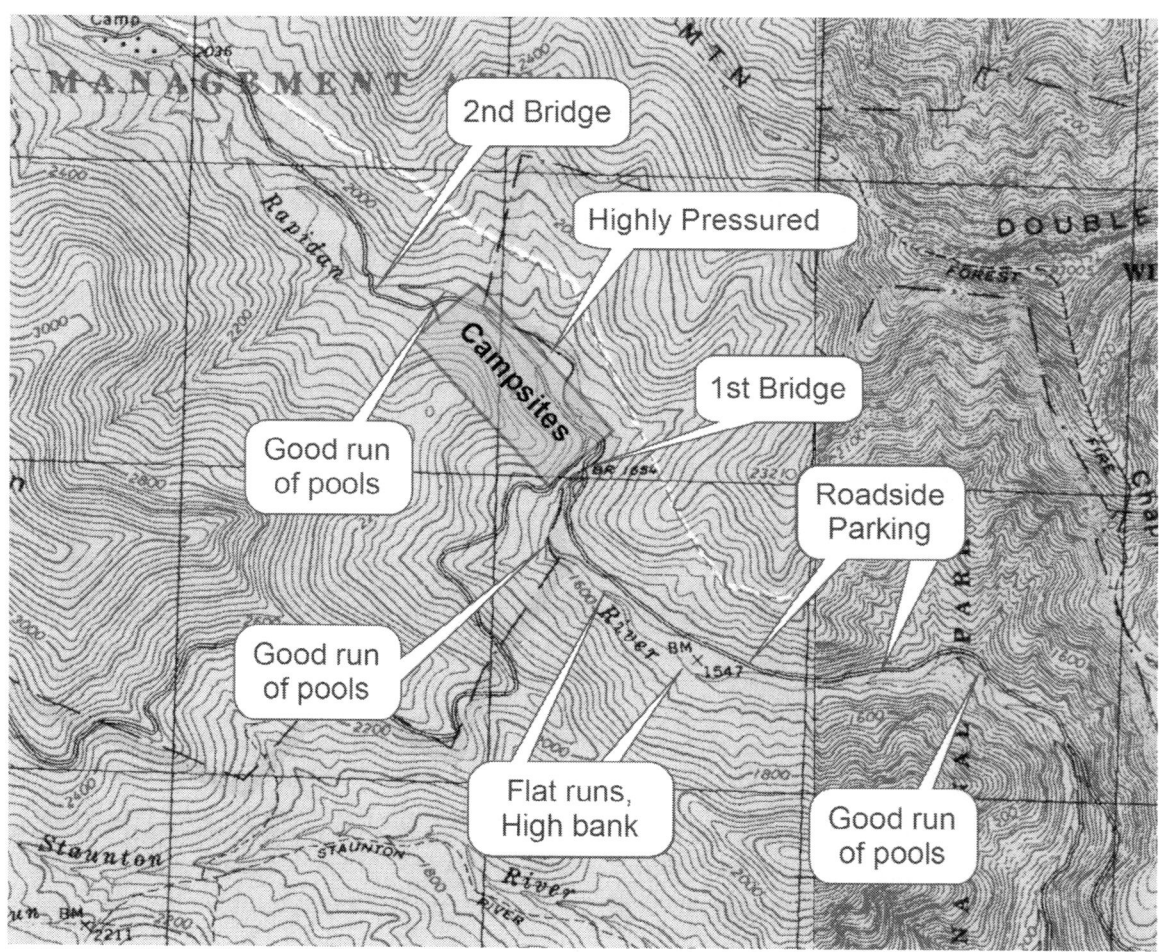

The key difference between going up or downstream is pressure. Upstream of the bridge, there are an infinite number of campsites that extend all the way up to and just beyond the second bridge. Therefore, the better fishing is downstream of the first bridge.

Upstream

In spite of the engaging panorama on the right as you cross the first bridge, you are entering the second most heavily pressured section of the upper Rapidan. The first clue is the large camp area that stretches off to the left. Every turn to the right between bridge 1 and 2 leads to another campsite on the river. The pressure does not abate until you move up the hill leading away from the campsite complex at the second bridge.

Given that, you may as well park anywhere off to the right. If you pull into one of the early campsites, you will get to fish up the hill that leads to a huge red clay cliff. The river creates a stairstep pattern with the water running in a narrow channel between small rocks and boulders. There are decent numbers of fallen logs stretched across the river to create holding areas for trout. As you move around the bend away from the red cliff, there are some good shallow "lakes" upstream. Look for the darker shade of green to determine where the main channel lays.

Beyond that, the river scatters across a wide boulder strewn, gentle downward pitch that is not worth fishing. Immediately above the pitch, there are some good holes next to large rocks on the left, but you are beginning to enter the "campsite zone." Once you realize you are in that zone, you may as well just walk until the last campsite is behind you in the vicinity of 38.47460, -78.38530. From there until you reach bridge 2, the river returns to the look and feel you experienced downstream of the bridge culminating in the same type of ideal, deep pool at 38.47483, -78.38618. This is a difficult pool to fish with a large log stretched across the river obstructing your approach. Once you finish, leave the river because you are within sight of the bridge and the campsite complex just upstream. It's a steep climb to get out of the river, but there are plenty of handholds to moderate the difficulty.

The view from the first bridge looking north has been photographed countless times.

Drive up the road, park and walk over to the stream to discover a gentle, shallow meander across a wide bed.

Even though this is near all the campsites, that does not mean the walking is easy.

The best pool of the stretch is at the upper end.

It is followed by the next best pool just upstream.   Exit after fishing this spot.

Downstream

Driving north from where Quaker Run road intersects the river, the Rapidan presents a complicated and troubling dilemma. Where to pull over? You catch glimpses of the river through the thick trees and tight brush as you drive north serenaded by the river's dull roar if you have your window down. However, in many locations, the road veers away from the river; giving rise to a fisherman's panic of missing good water. The simple answer is that you are. The entire river from the intersection up to the first bridge is prime water.

The first thing to note is that the river flattens out in this section. Downstream from the Quaker Run parking lot, it featured dramatic plunge pools and massive boulders as the river dropped precipitously, losing elevation to bottom out at the Graves Mill parking lot far below. The river takes a rest from its downward hurdle in this section. It widens out as it pushes through a temporary valley that is approximately 1.4 miles long. Instead of huge boulders and dramatic rocks, the typical picture is one of a gently flowing stream framed by high banks and medium sized chunks of rock. There are places where the boulders become large and movement can be difficult given the compression of the banks and the lack of a defined path.

The best pools nestle below gradient breaks created by medium sized rocks stretched across the river like gigantic pearl necklaces. However, you should be cautious as you walk up the shallow runs between the pools. Many of these have a deep channel or a small, deep pocket behind a strategically placed rock where fish hold. My experience is that many anglers who fish the upper Rapidan skip from pool to pool and ignore the good water that exists between. Identify the deeper channels by the slightly darker shade of green and you will pick up plenty of fish that have not seen a fly or a lure all season.

Most people find a place to park with the intent of fishing downstream from where the road intersects the river in the vicinity of 38.46492, -78.36960 to the Quaker Run parking area. At that point, the river takes a sharp U-turn to pitch north and then retreats south as it enters a transition zone of increased elevation loss and the associated higher number of plunge pools leading back down to the parking area. I prefer fishing upstream from this point. Pick a spot anywhere along the road and bushwhack to the river. In fact, the farther you have to walk, the better the fishing will be. A good place to pull off is near 38.46635, -78.38095. Walking for a distance as little as 50 yards can be enough to discourage 50% of the anglers.

Once on the river, note that the bottom is covered with boulders with the minimum amount of sand. There's good gravel to sustain the mountain insects and the trees form a protective canopy that keeps the river cool enough to sustain life during the hot Virginia summers. Early in the morning, you can enjoy nature's light show with the leaves glowing in infinite shades of green as the sun punches through the canopy. The banks are high between the entry point and 38.46798, -78.38423 and you should plan to stay in the river for that entire half mile stretch. The key feature is the 30 foot bank that will appear on the right as a river takes a slight swing to the left. It marks the start of the good fishing leading up to the first bridge.

Just as it is with cereal where the prize is always at the bottom of the box, the biggest and best pool below the bridge is at the end of the hike. There is a pool that has to be at least 10 feet deep bordered by a steep rock wall on the right and framed by fallen logs in the vicinity of 38.46798, -78.38423. Save that spot for the end because you need to be in perfect form by the time you reach it to be able to cast around the logs. Once you finish with this pool, fish upstream around the corner and then walk back to the road. At that point, you are close enough to the bridge for the pressure to keep fish in a constant state of "spook."

Park at any of the turnouts and walk to the river.   The valley floor levels out below the bridge and allows the water to spread out.

The banks are steep - you have to pick your entry and exit points.

Note the dense tree cover that keeps the water cool in the summer.

The best two pools are near the bridge.

Go deep in both - the fish are smart enough to hug the bottom.

Bottom Line

The downstream stretch is another wonderful section on the upper Rapidan. It's a little bit easier physically since there is not a significant amount of elevation gain. The flatness of the valley makes for easier walking and the lack of large boulders minimizes the climbing. Upstream, you encounter many campsites that overlook the river. If you are unaware of this on your first visit, you'll be startled by a cheery hello from the bank and feel a bit silly if you were sneaking up the river to avoid spooking the fish when you see folks sitting around cooking hot dogs and kids running around being kids. With the exception of the single spot downstream of bridge 2 at 38.47483, -78.38618, I recommend you not bother to fish between bridges 1 and 2.

Upper Rapidan (2nd Bridge)

Google Map Coordinates: 38.46257,-78.365602

Summary Rating

Parking	Red	Spin Fishing	Red
Canoe/Kayak Launch	Red	Fly Fishing	Yellow
Distance to River	Yellow	Trout	Green
Can Bike to River	Red	Smallmouth Bass	Red
Physical Fitness	Red	Pressure	Green
Scenery	Green	Overall	Green

By the time you reach the area above the second bridge, the Rapidan enters a steep canyon that provides an effective filter to pressure. It's hard rock climbing to move upstream from the second bridge. Likewise, the pools become small and problematic for those who rely on spin gear. Spin anglers will end up doing a healthy amount of walking to find a pool large and deep enough to allow the spinner to activate. Your best bet from the second bridge north is to use fly gear.

Special Regulations

"Only single-point hook artificial lures may be used-no bait. On those streams open to harvest, the creel limit is 6 trout per day with a 9-inch minimum size for brook trout and a 7-inch minimum size for brown and rainbow trout. On all other streams open to fishing, catch and release regulations apply. The release of any brown trout back into any Park stream is prohibited and brown trout less than 7 inches must be disposed of within the Park but away from Park streams, roads or trails. This is an effort to limit the impacts of brown trout on the native brook trout populations. Contact the Shenandoah National Park at 540-999-3500 for the annual list of streams open to harvest." - VDGIF

The Rapidan is not on the list of streams open to harvest. It is strictly catch and release.

Getting to the Stream

North: From US 29 continue south past Culpeper. Turn Right at Hoover Road (VA 609) and follow it towards Syria. Turn right at North Blue Ridge Turnpike (VA 231) to go north, continuing towards Syria. Take the first left onto Old Blue Ridge Turnpike (VA 670) at a "Y" in the road near an old grocery. Follow VA 670 for a little over 4 miles to Quaker Run Road. Turn left onto Quaker Run and follow it to the river.

North: From US 29, turn left onto South Main Street at Madison. Make a slight left onto North Blue Ridge Turnpike (VA 231) to go north, continuing towards Syria. Take the first left onto Old Blue Ridge Turnpike (VA 670) at a "Y" in the road near an old grocery. Follow VA 670 for a little over 4 miles to Quaker Run Road. Turn left onto Quaker Run and follow it to the river.

The road parallels the river. Continue past the first and second bridge and park on the north side of the second bridge at any of several campsites. I personally prefer to go farther up the hill and park in the single car slot to the left across from a tree that has the number 10 attached to it (38.48028, -78.39493). The second place to stop is at the gate itself. Both locations are near the best places to fish between the bridge and the gate (38.48789, -78.40621) that marks the entry back into the Shenandoah National Park and the road up to Camp Hoover.

Environment and Fish

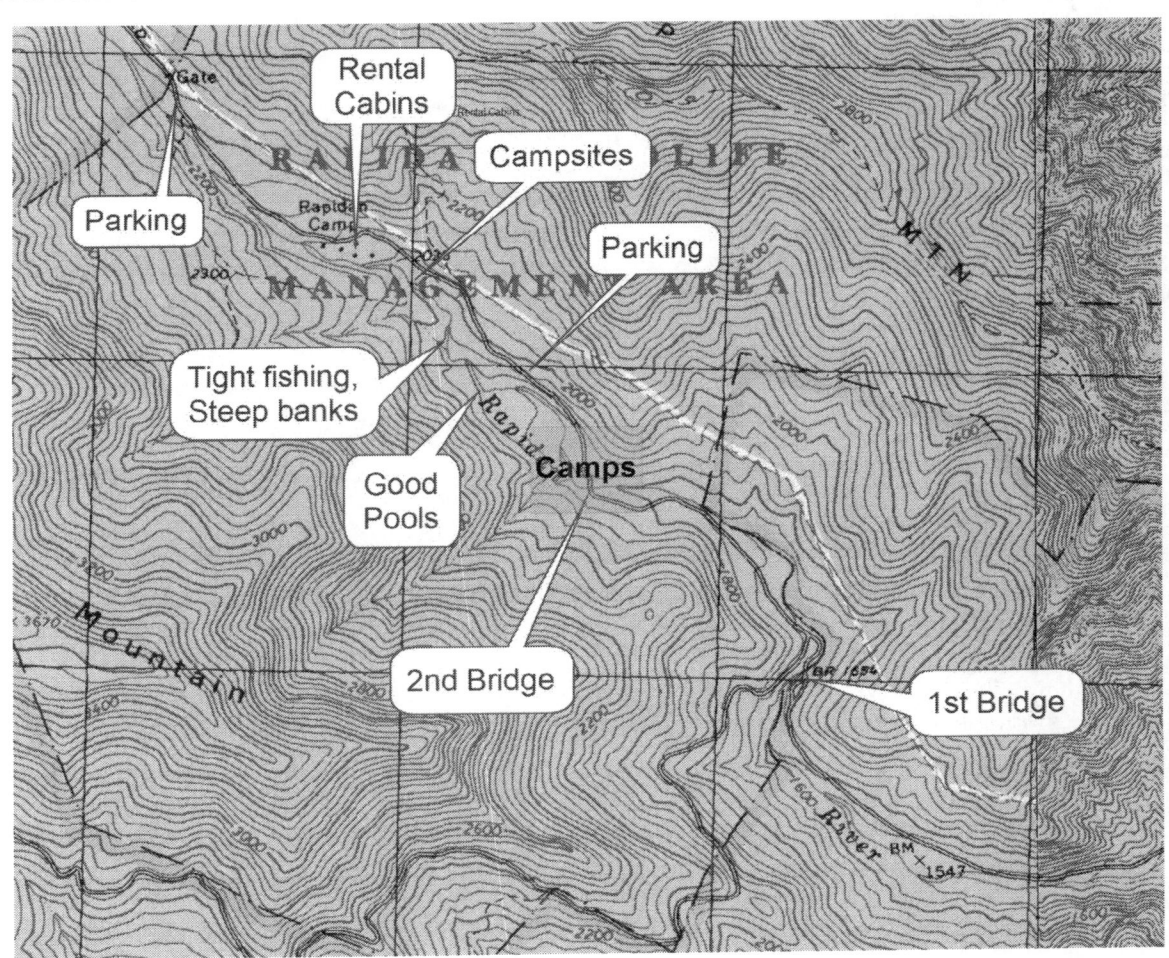

Why make a distinction between the two spots? The answer is simple. There is an improved camping area, with wooden cabins, that sits between the two. The cabins are privately owned by a club (www.RapidanCamps.org), and they rent them to non-members on a space available basis. At the boundary of the cabin area, there are additional primitive public campsites. All of this adds up to increased pressure. So, why not go where most people will not go because of the difficulty associated with reaching the river? Both of the sections discussed are in canyons that offer limited entry and exit. You need to be prepared to stay in the river for a third of a mile or more before encountering an opportunity to escape. The canyon leading into Camp Hoover, the second place I discuss, has more exit points than the first.

First Canyon

After crossing the second bridge, your first opportunity to enter the gorge is immediately to the left where there is a campsite at the water's edge. If you start fishing here, you will fish over the top of everyone who has camped within the last three weeks. Given that, I prefer to drive farther north on the rough road until I see the number 10 painted on a tree on the right. Pull off at the next turnout to the left and follow the faint trail that tumbles down the hill to the banks of the river at 38.47960, -78.39546. In spite of the good-looking water in front of you, do not start fishing. Walk downstream until you reach a pool complex at 38.47874, -78.39429. In my insane fisherman's mental calculus, that location is far enough upstream from the campsite complex to mark the boundary of the good fishing.

This is below the canyon and you can move back up to the road easily if you wish. Fish the pool complex and begin to walk upriver. There is no path and the underbrush grows thick all the way down to the bank. You are limited to walking at the edge of the river or snaking through the bushes and small saplings along the bank. Given that this is wild trout water, you want to avoid walking close to the streambed as much as possible. The guides at Mossy Creek Fly Fishing in Harrisonburg, Virginia have come up with a way to mitigate this situation if you are fishing with a friend. They recommend that the first angler approach the pool using dry flies. After working the water with dries, that angler quietly moves farther upstream to the next pool. The second angler fishes the same water using nymphs or streamers. By switching presentation, each angler has the opportunity to catch fish. Periodically throughout the day, switch rods so both can fish using different techniques. You can even do this between pools if you like.

Other than being in the canyon, there is nothing distinctive about this section of the river that deserves special comment. As you would expect, large rocks create pools on the downstream side. The pools are connected by drops in elevation where the river runs down staircases -- usually with the flow compressed and tightened. Rather than skip the staircases out of hand, at least throw a glance at them to ensure that there is not a holding area embedded in the feature. All it takes is a foot or two of calm water to make a trout happy. Most people will not bother to take the time to fish those spots. If you are using a Tenkara fly rod (no reel, just line), it's easy to drop a fly in small locations and you will catch more fish.

As you climb farther up the river, the rocks become larger and progress more difficult. You can use this to your advantage by hiding behind the rocks on the downstream side to minimize exposure to the fish upstream. Poke your head and casting arm above the boulder and target the broader pool above. There are some easy walking sections where the river broadens out where you can get a "long" cast, but most of your day will be tight fishing with a typical cast being 15 feet.

Enjoy the canyon until you reach a massive boulder complex near 38.48191, -78.39618. These are big rocks! You can't miss it! That spot marks the end of your fishing since there is a campsite approximately 50 yards upstream. That campsite is at the boundary of the Rapidan Camp area with the rental cabins. It is in this area you encounter additional anglers since it is an easy amble from the campsite into the canyon. You will not have a problem leaving the canyon to return to the road and walk back to your vehicle.

Walk down the path until you find the wide pools framed by large boulders.

Unlike farther upstream, the channel is deep here.

The rocks give you the opportunity to sneak up and attack from above.

The terrain can only be described as dramatic.

Each major elevation drop creates a deep pool.

Note the fisherman (right side of the picture) is dwarfed by the size of the massive rocks that frame the stream.

Second Canyon

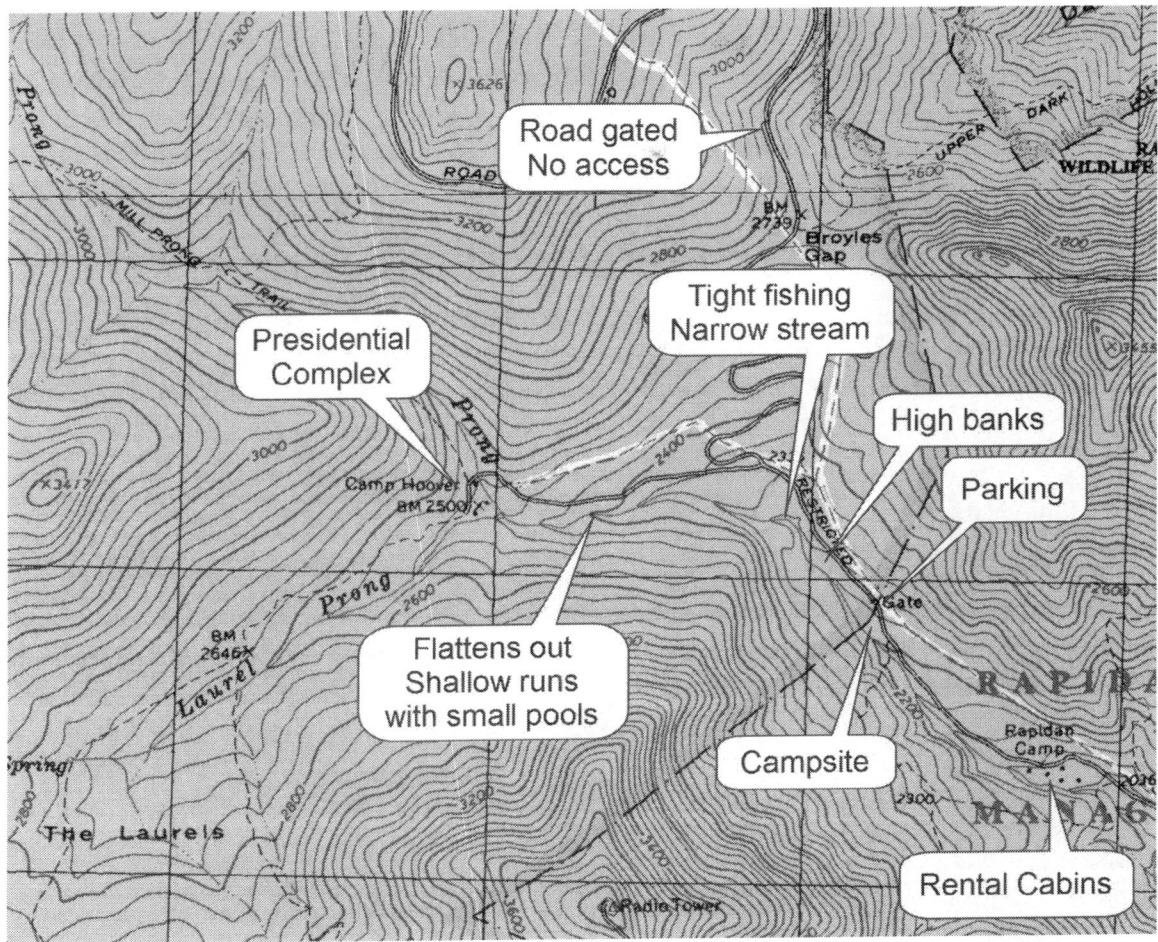

Skip through the area near the Rapidan Camp and drive up to the gate that marks the entrance to the Shenandoah National Park. Don't be discouraged if there are multiple cars parked near the gate. Many of these belong to hikers who trudge the 1 mile on the easy road to visit Camp Hoover.

Even though there is a campsite near the river at the end of the obvious trail from the parking area, the river upstream receives light pressure. The reason is that the fishing is technical and difficult. At this point, you are high in the Blue Ridge and getting closer and closer to the headwaters of the Rapidan. The Laurel Prong and Mill Prong streams combine only a mile upriver to create the Rapidan River. Therefore, the water is smaller, the streambed is tighter, and the trees are closer. In a good spot, the stream is 10 feet wide. On rare occasions, it extends out to 20 feet, but mostly is very narrow. The high banks close in on each side and limit your mobility. You will use your hands to work your way upstream over and around the boulders and between the trees. If you choose your spot, you can climb out on the right-hand side to bushwhack your way back to the road that leads to either the gate (turn right) or Camp Hoover (turn left).

The best approach is to fish up the river from the start point until the river takes a sharp left turn at a high, dirt covered cliff face in the vicinity of 38.49043, -78.41007. There's good fishing above and below that spot. Between the bend and Camp Hoover, the river runs significantly flatter with pools that are generally bigger and deeper. If you are using spin gear, this is the section you want to target. You should walk up the road until it forks at 38.492093,-78.410454. Backtrack 200 feet to 38.490682,-78.408673 and cut west through the brush until you reach the river. Fly rodders can fish the entire stretch.

The farther upstream you go, the skinnier the water gets. But... that said... there are still plenty of fish in any pool that has a spot at least a foot deep.

Narrow runs lead to small pools. Spin fishermen will find this impossible to fish.

One of the few broad spots in the stream.

This is rugged country. Do not attempt to fish here unless you are physically capable.

The work pays off when you hit spots like this.

Tight spots demand good casting accuracy.

Bottom Line

I like this section since it is remote. This is beyond the point where you can drive a vehicle and the fact that you have to walk into a difficult canyon where movement requires using hands as much as using feet, speaks volumes for light pressure. However, the water is smaller and the pools are fewer. The trout do not seem to mind and I routinely catch eight inch trout in this section.

Upper Rapidan (Camp Hoover)

Google Map Coordinates: 38.46257,-78.365602

Summary Rating

Parking	Red	Spin Fishing	Red
Canoe/Kayak Launch	Red	Fly Fishing	Red
Distance to River	Red	Trout	Green
Can Bike to River	Red	Smallmouth Bass	Red
Physical Fitness	Red	Pressure	Green
Scenery	Green	Overall	Red

The small feeder streams, Laurel Prong and Mill Prong, represent the ultimate in technical fishing. There is very little water, the pools (with two exceptions) are small and the vegetation surrounding the stream is oppressive. This makes fishing difficult and, when combined with the hike to reach the camp, pushes the rating to Red overall.

Special Regulations

"Only single-point hook artificial lures may be used-no bait. On those streams open to harvest, the creel limit is 6 trout per day with a 9-inch minimum size for brook trout and a 7-inch minimum size for brown and rainbow trout. On all other streams open to fishing, catch and release regulations apply. The release of any brown trout back into any Park stream is prohibited and brown trout less than 7 inches must be disposed of within the Park but away from Park streams, roads or trails. This is an effort to limit the impacts of brown trout on the native brook trout populations. Contact the Shenandoah National Park at 540-999-3500 for the annual list of streams open to harvest." - VDGIF

The Rapidan is not on the list of streams open to harvest. It is strictly catch and release.

Getting to the Stream

North: From US 29 continue south past Culpeper. Turn Right at Hoover Road (VA 609) and follow it towards Syria. Turn right at North Blue Ridge Turnpike (VA 231) to go north, continuing towards Syria. Take the first left onto Old Blue Ridge Turnpike (VA 670) at a "Y" in the road near an old grocery. Follow VA 670 for a little over 4 miles to Quaker Run Road. Turn left onto Quaker Run and follow it to the river.

South: From US 29, turn left onto South Main Street at Madison. Make a slight left onto North Blue Ridge Turnpike (VA 231) to go north, continuing towards Syria. Take the first left onto Old Blue Ridge Turnpike (VA 670) at a "Y" in the road near an old grocery. Follow VA 670 for a little over 4 miles to Quaker Run Road. Turn left onto Quaker Run and follow it to the river.

The road parallels the river. Follow it over the first and second bridge all the way to where it dead ends at the gate (38.48762,-78.40631). Park on the left where there are two small turnouts that will hold four vehicles.

Follow the road north to a fork approximately 0.4 miles from the gate (38.49203,-78.41068). Take the left hand fork and hike west another 0.6 miles until you reach Camp Hoover.

Environment and Fish

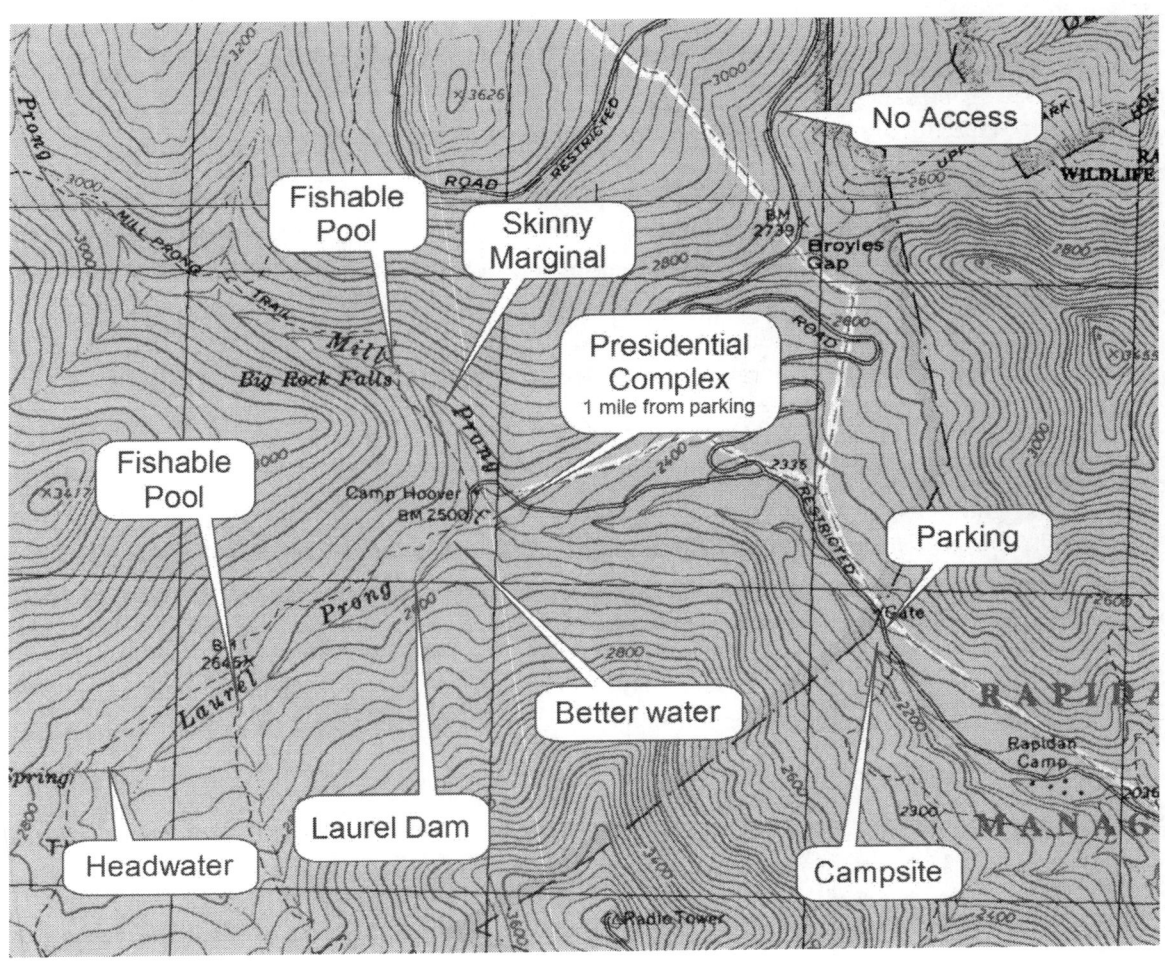

Other than the history associated with Camp Hoover, there is not much to recommend in terms of fishing. If you find yourself fishing the second canyon discussed in the previous chapter, you may as well walk the additional distance to Camp Hoover just to check it out. This is where President Hoover spent time in the summer; much as current Presidents spend it at Camp David. When you think back to the 1920-1930s, it had to take a day to get here from the Washington DC area. Hard to believe a President could be that out of touch. Clearly, our lives have been polluted by blackberries, constant e-mail and cell phones. If you come here, you will be out of touch since there is no cell phone coverage and can fish carefree and undistracted -- so maybe President Hoover had it right.

Laurel Prong

After walking the extra distance to the junction of Mill and Laurel Prongs, looking at the buildings and reading the information, you realize you have a fishing rod in your hand and wonder where you can use it. A logical thought might be to investigate wild trout on the two streams that create the headwaters of the Rapidan. One of the things that jumped out at me when I stood in front of the wooden panel that had a large map of the historic area was that the Camp derived its drinking water from a dam upstream on the Laurel Prong. A dam sounded good; promising a large body of water and potentially large fish. With that, I made my decision to fish the Laurel Prong.

Don't make the mistake I did. Be alert! The map is not specific on where the dam is. I continued to walk up the trail that led to the west hoping to find a marked trail pointing to the dam and the stream. While there are some trails that lead to the stream, none led to the dam. If you detour on the first trail to the left, it leads to a relatively wide spot in the stream that is worth fishing. (38.48543,-78.42933). Eventually, I walked over a mile to stand staring at the small trickle of water that was the absolute headwater of the mighty Rapidan River. Other than thinking to myself that it was pretty cool to see that, I still wanted to find the fish.

I returned to the map and realized that the trail to the Laurel Dam was next to the sign. Follow the path along the irrigation ditch, framed with a stone wall, until the path veers away to the south. Eventually it leads to the stream and a small sign proclaiming you have reached the Laurel Dam (38.48833,-78.42376).

If the sign was not there, you would not think you were any place special. There was no dam that I could see, just a slightly wider spot in the river. I guess that "back in the day" when this was a critical water source for the Camp, it was better maintained and held more water.

The stream is better to fish moving downstream from the dam rather than up and that is the direction I recommend you go. There are two pools immediately below the dam that merit attention. They also indicate the challenge you are about to face. The Rapidan River is no longer a river at this point. In fact, it hasn't really been a "river" since you walked west from Camp Hoover. It is a trickle of water that has collected in various holding areas with the stream velocity dictated by the amount of rainfall and seepage from the springs high on the side of the mountain. While the banks are not drastically elevated, they overhang the stream enough to create problems for any type of casting. With the exception of one wide spot approximately one hundred yards up from Camp Hoover, there is no place to throw a spinner and even fishing with a fly is a challenge.

The bridge leads to the camp. Amazing to think you can sit on the same deck that Hoover did.

This is the confusing map. Follow the trail in front of it (in back of you as you look at the sign) to the dam.

The sign happily announces your arrival at the dam.

Otherwise, you would not know you are there. This is it....

Fishing downstream from the dam is a challenge. Tight, small pools protected by all sorts of stream junk.

Painfully narrow as the creek staggers down to the camp.

And... for those of you who walk the additional mile up the headwaters, this is the best you can expect for fishable water.

It's not really worth it to move much beyond the camp or the dam.

Mill Prong

As marginal as Laurel Prong is, Mill Prong is worse since it is the smaller of the two streams. Granted, this high up in the mountain, you should not have great expectations for a huge volume of water. The Rapidan needs input from all of the feeder streams to create the volume that allows trout to survive the warm Virginia summers. At the junction with Laurel Prong, Mill Prong actually looks promising. The stream is approximately 10 to 15 feet wide and plunges through a moderately steep elevation drop; hinting of pools upstream. Cross the bridge and walk up the path past the presidential quarters, known as the Brown House, until you get to the road crossing at 38.491814,-78.420467. Between the junction and this crossing, the stream runs close to several of the buildings associated with Camp Hoover.

While the history is fascinating, the fishing is not. At the road crossing, you are at the upper end of the "good" section of Mill Prong. You can follow the Mill Prong trail north along the left bank of the stream. If you venture into the stream, the fishable water is widely spread and protected by dense, overhanging vegetation. If you are a true trout addict, you may want to walk the 0.4 miles uphill to reach "Big Rock Falls" (38.49543,-78.42397). Don't expect Niagara Falls. Big Rock Falls is an abrupt drop of 15 feet across a flat rock surface. The falls terminates in a circular pool approximately 20 feet wide and two or three feet deep that holds fish even at the height of summer. You can attack the pool by cautiously approaching from the south, staying in the streambed, or follow the trail across the stream and slither in from the right-hand side using the vegetation at the edge of the falls to shield your approach.

It's definitely not worth walking any farther upstream at this point. Just like on Laurel Prong, Mill Prong emanates from several small springs a third of a mile north of the falls. The springs create three feeder creeks that combine to create the minimal water volume in Mill Prong, but they are intermittent and do not reliably pump out a significant amount of water.

At this point, you have fished all there is to fish in the vicinity of Camp Hoover. Walk back, enjoy the history and then move farther downriver to get into some better fish!

Mill Prong at summer low at the bridge.

But... it does not get any better upstream.

Exceptionally small pools, tight vegetation.

I could not fish this... too hard.

The only thing worth walking up Mill Prong for is the falls. There is a large pool that is also a popular swimming hole for hikers in the summer.

See www.swimmingholes.org - yes, there is a website for everything.

Bottom Line

I recommend you not waste time fishing in the area of Camp Hoover unless you also want to visit it for the historical significance. There is just not enough water to make a special trip worthwhile. Your fishing experience ends at the junction of Mill and Laurel Prongs. From there down, the Rapidan River is a river that has enough fish and water to make for a productive and enjoyable day. Upstream from Camp Hoover, it's just sweaty exercise.

Gear Guide

Given the fact that fishing on the Rapidan includes both bass and trout, you need a range of gear that will handle both types of fish. In the lower Rapidan, be prepared to hook up with a feisty 20 inch smallmouth monster while the equivalent trout lurking in a cold pool, high on a mountainside will be 9 inches long.

You probably have everything you need right now. Even though I subscribe to the theory that if you know how many fishing rods you have, you do not have enough - a philosophy that can get you in trouble with a non-fishing spouse/partner. Compare what you currently own with the recommendations below and if it's close enough, then you're good to go and can save your relationship.

As I developed my recommendations, I looked for the best value. However, I need to admit up front that I'm not an expert. I do not have a laboratory full of equipment where I conduct extensive tests on every aspect of each piece of equipment mentioned. Rather, this is what I use after fishing for over 50 years on a limited budget. I need to qualify "limited budget." There is a minimum set of requirements that gear needs to meet to give years of reliable service. Otherwise, you will end up replacing it time and time again. Therefore, I won't recommend the economical starter kits found in many major department stores because I assume that anyone who reads this book has already decided that they enjoy fishing and will have moved beyond that level of gear. The starter kits are an inexpensive way for novices to test the waters and assess their enjoyment of the sport - but not a good baseline for years of hard use.

Fly Fishing

As a general statement, I am an avid supporter of the gear designed and manufactured by Fly Fishing Benefactors (FFB), an Internet only retailer (www.flyfishingbenefactors.com). In addition to producing high-quality gear at a very reasonable price, this company donates a considerable amount of their gross profit to various charitable organizations. FFB has manufactured branded gear in support of Project Healing Waters, a group dedicated to rehabilitating disabled veterans, the Virginia Fly Fishing Festival and others.

That said, if you prefer to buy from a traditional brick-and-mortar fly shop like Mossy Creek, Urban Angler or Albemarle Angler or a "big box" operation like Bass Pro Shop, Gander Mountain, LL Bean or Orvis, take this list and use it as a guide.

Bass Water

The minimum weight rod you should use for smallmouth is a 5/6 wt that is over 8 feet long. Since the typical smallmouth bass on the Rapidan is 16 inches or under, you do not need to "up gun" to a 7/8 wt.

Granted, bigger fish demand bigger lures and bigger lures require thicker line that is thrown by a heavier weight rod. Unless you need a large rod for some other purpose, then save your money. Besides, with all the sunfish and smaller bass that will slam into your fly, you'll have more fun using lighter gear.

The FFB 5/6 wt San Juan rod represents a tremendous value. It matches up against the rods by major manufacturers and is made out of better quality graphite. The San Juan uses IM8 graphite that is lighter and stiffer than the IM6 normally used in rods at this price point ($140 in late 2010). What's the advantage of the better graphite? Fly Anglers Online had the best explanation (my bold):

"When you increase the modulus of the graphite, you increase the ability of that graphite to store and release energy. You also increase the speed that the rod releases the stored energy. That in turn, increases the line speed that is generated in the cast. Increase **the modulus, and you increase the reaction speed and power of the rod blank.**

Unfortunately, increased modulus results in increased costs. The process involved in creating higher modulus graphite is a costly one. The highest modulus graphite material costs as much as ten times more than standard graphite."

Given that, it is amazing that FFB can upgrade everyone to IM8 quality graphite and keep the cost as low as they do. Everything else about a fly rod is just looks since most of the other components are fairly standard. That said, the FFB includes upgraded Portuguese cork, a walnut seat and aluminum lockups.

Once you have your rod, you need a decent reel tuned to the rod. The reel should hold the appropriate weight fly line, with backing, matched to the rod and balance when you hold it at the grip. Your arms will be sore after a full day of fishing with an out-of-balance rod/reel combination. No matter how fancy a reel gets, all it does is hold line. It will be a rare and exciting day if you get a fish "on the reel " and actually have to use the drag. Therefore, choosing a reel boils down to how light do you want it to be and how much money do you want to spend?

FFB manufactures several lines of reels. The inexpensive, lightweight Deschutes II reel offers great looks at an exceptional price. It roughly compares with the mid-arbor from another major manufacturer in terms of performance with the "major" being slightly lighter at the expense of a narrower diameter. The larger diameter on the Deschutes allows it to hold more line. Both have centerline disc drags, one-way clutch bearings and glass composite drag surfaces. Having used both reels, the performance is comparable – so go with the best value – the Deschutes. It was running $99 in late 2010.

If you have additional money to spend, you can move up the feature ladder where the reels become lighter and fancier/cooler looking as a result of the additional machining to remove more metal. But the bottom line is that a reel such as the Deschutes II is all you really need. If you really need to conserve cash, FFB has two very inexpensive, low end reels – the Rapidan and the Madison – that run about $40 and $20 respectively.

Trout Water

If you have the extra money to spend, you should buy a 2 wt rod to use on the trout section of the Rapidan. Any of the fly shops noted in the next chapter can give you advice on this type of rod. Since a large Rapidan brook trout is 9 inches, you don't need much in terms of heavy artillery to land a fish of that size. Another option is to depart from tradition and pick up one of the new TenkaraUSA rods from Mossy Creek Fly Fishing (a local Virginia distributor).

The problem with buying a 2 wt is that it is not much good anywhere outside of a mountain stream. A normal size stocked trout on any of the other nearby Virginia waters such as Passage Creek, the Rose, Robinson and Hughes Rivers will overmatch a 2 wt. In addition, 2 wt line will not be up to throwing normal size streamers required to attract the attention of a stocker. Therefore, a 2 wt is a luxury – get one if you can afford it, but you don't need one to successfully fish the trout section of the Rapidan.

You can use a Tenkara anywhere you are comfortable using 5X or thinner tippet while recognizing the limitation associated with only being able to cast 20 to 30 feet since there is no reel with this type of rod. I used Tenkara rods successfully in the mountains as well as the Rose River and the Dan River in southern Virginia, catching trout up to 16 inches, and it is my tool of choice when I know every cast will be short.

However, unlike me, who successfully snuck the Tenkara into the house without my wife knowing about it (it is only 20 inches long when fully collapsed), you may not have that luxury. Whatever you do, don't make the mistake I made - I covertly amassed plenty of fly fishing "stuff" without being challenged until I put it everything in the basement one winter to clean it. Once she saw the accumulated stack, I had some tough questions to answer.

Therefore, to avoid a similar situation, I recommend you get a 3/4 wt and use it as your standard trout rod. If you know you're going to spend more time on the small streams, load it with a 3 wt line; otherwise put on 4 wt. A 4 wt will allow you throw heavier flies when you need to.

FFB wins again in terms of price-performance. I highly recommend their satin green Shenandoah rod (picture shows the color actually matches a Shenandoah fern for maximum camouflage). A few years ago, they gave me a loaner to test and I immediately fell in love with it. Since I had to give it back when the test was complete, I decided that it needed an extended test that persisted for two full years before I wrote my formal review of this great tool.

I put my money where my mouth was and bought two of them - one for myself and another for my brother as a welcome home gift upon his return from a tour of duty in Afghanistan with the Screaming Eagles of the 101st Airborne. You don't give a combat hardened, airborne-ranger infantryman a piece of garbage!

Like its heavier brother, the San Juan, the Shenandoah features the identical IM8 graphite with fast action. It has all the same bells and whistles in terms of upgraded cork handle, walnut seat as well as aluminum lockups. At 3.3 ounces, it is one of the lightest you will find at the amazing price point of approximately $120 as of late 2010.

Here is the Shenandoah rod with the FFB Snake I reel in action on the upper Rose River. Yes, I fell victim to the great looks of the Snake - it has a high-capacity spool that is 3.27 inches in diameter yet only weighs 3.54 ounces. It will hold 50 yards of 20 pound backing or over 70 yards of 10 pound backing with a standard 4 wt fly line.

Follow the same logic on choosing a reel as you did for bass. Unfortunately, there is a breakpoint between 4 wt and anything heavier. The reels designed to hold the lighter line are smaller - appropriate given the corresponding lighter weight of the rod and the less demanding fish you intend to attach to the other end. For that reason, I recommend you not get a single reel with an extra spool and put bass line on one and trout line on the other. Get a separate reel for your trout rod.

My recommendation remains the same. Get the Deschutes I or equivalent. Spending more than that moves you to greater style and lighter weight; nice, but not vital. That said, that Snake reel is beautiful and surely impressed those mountain trout!

Backup Solution

Unlike the spin rods I discuss below, fly rods are delicate instruments. Regardless of the manufacturer, graphite is only so tough. If you whack a rod on a rock as you stumble to get to that great spot on the upper Rapidan, you could put a nick in the graphite that makes it snap on your next cast. At the end of the mile hike into Hunting Run or 3.5 miles downstream from Elys Ford, you do not want to lose your ability to fish!

Any time you walk farther from your vehicle than you are willing to backtrack if your equipment fails, you need to bring a backup. Since fly reels rarely, if ever fail, all you need is a compact, backup fly rod that can be dual purposed to keep you fishing whether you are hunting bass or trout.

The FFB pack rod in a natural setting...
the tailgate of my truck

The industry has a solution - the travel or pack rod. Orvis, LL Bean and Fly Fishing Benefactors all have solutions in the 5 wt class. 5 wt sits perfectly in the middle between the 4 wt rod used for trout and the 6 wt rod for bass.

A 5 wt rod will do just fine throwing 4 wt or 6 wt line - allowing you to use the reel from the failed rod and not have to haul around yet another piece of backup gear. As of late 2010, the price ranged from approximately $160 for the FFB rod up to $200 for the Orvis version.

If you don't think you need a backup rod you can put in your day pack, think again. Regardless of the manufacturer, pack rods are so light that they do not add to the physical stress of a day of fishing and will save your day when the unthinkable happens. Go ahead and plan for the worst and don't get caught flat-footed, staring dumbly at a broken rod tip, realizing you have a mile to walk back to your vehicle for a replacement.

Spin Fishing

If you are a spin angler, your eyes glazed over when you read the advice for the fly guys. Hopefully, you skipped it and jumped right to here. Thankfully, the problem you have to solve is very simple given the proliferation of good gear at a reasonable price. Unfortunately, just like the fly rodder, your biggest decision will be "how much to spend?" If your adrenaline pumps and the money in your pocket starts to produce an overwhelming itch when you read the latest issue of Bassmaster Magazine, you may have a hard time with the minimum expectations I lay out below. That's fine. The purpose of this section is to stipulate the minimum, not the maximum.

Bass Water

in his book, *Pursuing River Smallmouth Bass,* Ken Penrod nets out the environment against which you must match your gear:

- Swift current
- Dense cover
- Big fish

With his point being that the ultralight gear many people favor because of the more violent feel it gives when playing most fish ends up being inadequate when there is a real beast on the end of the line. Given the aggressive, tough fight in many river smallmouth as small as 12 inches, you could quickly find your drag smoking to end with a pathetic "pop" that signifies your line just snapped off at the reel seat.

The bottom line on a rod is that it needs to be a graphite medium action. I'm sure there are people who will have different perspectives, but I love my Shakespeare Ugly Stik that is 5'10" and designed for 6 to 15 pound line (model SPL110). Prior to switching to the Ugly Stik brand, I broke several other rods in rapid succession by handling them improperly. As an aggressive fisherman, I'm not interested in gear that needs to be babied. The Stiks have held up well rattling around in the back of my truck as well as taking the brunt my weight as I routinely trip and slip in the boulder fields protecting the good spots. Ugly Stiks just won't die. The downside is that some more experienced anglers complain that the rods are less sensitive and heavier than other models.

The Stiks are made using a graphite core protected with a fiberglass ("E-glass") coating. Shakespeare stands behind these rods with a five year warranty. I took a quick look over at the Bass Pro Shop review to confirm that most users opinions match mine. Of the 115 reviews posted, 107 were favorable and would recommend the rod to a friend. Although I can't put my finger on it right now, I remember reading a review in Field & Stream where the editor tried to break one of these by hanging excessive amounts of weight from the end. He ran out of weight at 55 pounds and never killed the rod. These things just won't break.

You can get one or two piece Ugly Stiks. I prefer the one piece since I think it is more sensitive. Stiks cost around $30 as of late 2010.

I use Mitchell 308X reels for smallmouth bass. They have a fast retrieve (5.5 :1) making it easy to impart the necessary action to stimulate fishy interest. The drag may fade a bit at higher settings, but not enough to make me want to spend more money. In addition, the extra spool allows you to solve any "bird's nest" quickly. Finally, the 10 bearing drive makes this a very smooth performer. A Mitchell runs around $50 as of late 2010.

Trout Water

Stick with the Ugly Stiks for all the reasons mentioned above! I like the 4'6" ultralight rod that is tailored for 2 to 6 pound line (model SP1146 1UL). While Shakespeare makes other lengths of ultralight rods, I prefer the shortest because the tight water in the upper reaches of the Rapidan as well as the Staunton Rivers limits the room you have to cast. You may only have a few feet to flip your spinner into a small pool. You can buy one for just under $40 in late 2010. In effect, this particular rod is the equivalent of the special-purpose 2 wt fly rod I mentioned above. If you can only buy one rod to use on the typical mountain streams as well the nearby stocked rivers that have larger fish, you should up-gun to a 7 foot length.

Match the rod up with a Mitchell 310X reel and you have a dynamic combination to deal with small brook trout in the Shenandoah. The 310 series sports a fast 4.9:1 gear ratio and costs $60 in late 2010.

Other

Personal Communications

You will probably not be able to pick up your cell phone carrier in the mountains. You should plan on being out of communications and consider carrying a personal locator beacon (PLB) in case you have an accident. Remember those guys who died on Mt Rainer a few years ago? What about the NFL players on the overturned boat off Florida in 2009? They were alive for plenty of time, but the rescue team could not find them. When I read about these tragedies, it was a wakeup call for me as I routinely fish by myself when I cannot get anyone else to go. Personal locator beacons provide lifesaving emergency communications, but come at a price.

The cost issue reminds me of a conversation in a bicycle shop years ago when I wanted to purchase a helmet for my son and asked for his advice on what to get. The bike guy responded, "Does your son have a $10 head or a $100 head?" Geez...

I bought a GOOD helmet. So, is your life worth $99 bucks? That's what the Spot Messenger PLB is going for as I write this CatchGuide. The Spot PLB also allows you to sign up for a very inexpensive insurance policy that covers the cost of emergency evacuation. Get something.

Radio

The Rapidan is noisy. In places where it is quiet, you want to be quiet as well. if you spread out on the stream, you lose the ability to share what's working and what's not with your buddy unless you have a small FRS radio with you. There are some models advertised as waterproof, but if you look closely at the disclaimer associated with most of them, they are merely water resistant.

The ones that are truly waterproof are more expensive and put themselves out of the running based on that high cost. If you plan on getting wet, you need a radio rated against a standard that is called JIS7 or IPX7. For more information on the rating standards, visit www.hy-com.com/jis.htm. Therefore, I recommend you take the cheapest radios you can find and hope you don't fall into the river. If you make a splash, no big deal – just get another one when they go on sale or have a big rebate. Even an inexpensive radio has a decent range that allows you to stay in touch with the other members of your party. Given the nature of the river, you will not spread out more than a quarter mile, so you do not need extended range. In any case, if you separate much farther than that, you may not be able to communicate anyway – even if your FRS has a range of 20 miles - because of the "line of sight" limitation associated with FRS radios. "Line of sight" means that the radio will only work if there are no obstructions such as hills or mountains between you and the recipient of your communication.

Wild Animals

The Rapidan is wild... even in places close to civilization. You can encounter bears at the Confluence, Hunting Run or Elys Ford! Of course, the Shenandoah National Park is full of black bears with 1 per square kilometer (about 2.5 per square mile) according to one report I read. Regardless of the specific number, the Blue Ridge is famous for its high density of these animals. As such, you must exercise the appropriate amount of caution when it comes to wildlife.

When fishing in a remote area, I always carry bear spray. I know there are some people who believe that I am nuts for being overly cautious, but I would always rather be safe than sorry. In fact, after an encounter with a large dog when fishing on Great Seneca Creek in Gaithersburg, Maryland, I realized that I need to be prepared for encounters with all sorts of animals. Of course, the day you forget it is the day you need it.

Lon and I were fishing on the Rose River a few miles farther north of the Rapidan when I got a call on the radio from him telling me that he had just spooked the largest black bear he had ever seen and it was heading in my direction. I reached down to my hip to get the bear spray ready and realized I left it in the truck. I also carry a small air horn, so I pulled it out and bleated out a few loud honks in hopes of warning the bear and convincing it to change its direction. Thankfully, I did not see him, so it must have worked. If you don't want to carry bear spray, carry a loud noisemaker as a backup option.

There have been a number of studies conducted in Alaska confirming that a large canister of bear spray is a better option than carrying a weapon. I need to comment that the laws routinely change related to chemical sprays and before you carry bear spray or other chemical repellents, it is up to you to check that it is currently legal. A good first start is to check the website handgunlaw.us *for an unofficial opinion* and then check with your local authorities.

Guides / Fly Shops

Mossy Creek Fly Fishing

Mossy Creek Fly Fishing

1790 – 92 East Market St.
Harrisonburg, VA 22801
540 – 434 – 2444

Brian and Colby Trow

Website
www.mossycreekflyfishing.com

Mossy Creek Fly Fishing specializes in both wade and float trips for trout and smallmouth bass. They are equally comfortable floating down the James or Shenandoah rivers in pursuit of smallmouth bass and musky as they are cautiously wading in search of trout on mountain streams, spring creeks and freestone creeks that exist in the area. Their approach to guiding is to put you on catchable fish and to suggest flies and techniques that have proven effective on the waters being fished. The emphasis is on safety, enjoyment, and catching fish.

April through October is the prime season for float trips on the James and Shenandoah Rivers for smallmouth, largemouth, carp, and musky. Beyond smallies, the Shenandoah Valley boasts some of the best spring creek fishing in the country. Mossy Creek, Beaver Creek, and Smith Creek are only minutes from the shop. The guide service covers rivers, streams, spring creeks, and private waters from the George Washington National Forest across the valley floor to the Shenandoah National Park. Mossy also guides on Virginia's best delayed harvest and special regulation streams within an hour of the shop. The trout fishing can be excellent year round with a peak season between March and June.

Beyond the public water, Mossy Creek has arrangements with landowners who provide access to a large inventory of private water to include two sections of the fabulous Mossy Creek. While they do not guide on the Rapidan, they provide directions, advice and opinions on where to go and what will work - the same as they do for the broad-spectrum of trout and bass water on either side of the mountains.

Specifically, Mossy guides and manages River Valley Farm, Susie Q Farm, Stoney Creek at Wintergreen Resort, and two private stretches of Mossy Creek. Fishing pressure is kept to a minimum and all of the water is regulated as fly fishing only, catch and release, barbless fisheries.

River Valley can produce trout over 12 pounds and 32 inches or can be just plain BIG*; like the one I caught there - check out that smile*! Susie Q Farm and the private stretches of Mossy Creek produce some of the biggest brown trout in Virginia. Stoney Creek is only 45 minutes from Harrisonburg and has over 3 miles of some of the best brook trout fishing in the Mid-Atlantic.

Fly Fishing Classes: Mossy Creek has one of the most active fly fishing schools in Virginia; teaching hundreds of anglers annually in Harrisonburg and at the Wintergreen Resort. The school is Orvis Endorsed, provides all the equipment and conducts classes on private water. Classes take four hours and cover the use of rods, reels, and lines as well as choosing equipment to match different environments - lake, river, and salt water. Students learn about fly selection, leaders and knots. It all comes together on the water where the instructor can offer practical, personalized casting instruction and the student can catch fish.

For experienced anglers, the shop offers two hour casting clinics to tune up your technique.

Mossy Creek is along the I-81 corridor and is open six days a week. In addition to carrying a wide selection of gear from all of the top manufacturers, they are the regional distributor for TenkaraUSA; an emerging, innovative style of fly fishing that is perfect for mountain water.

The store is open Monday to Friday between 10AM and 6PM; Saturday 10AM to 5PM and closed Sunday.

Urban Angler

Urban Angler Ltd.

703 – 527 – 2524

Richard Farino

Website
www.urbanangler.com

The Urban Angler is a full service fly shop staffed with friendly, experienced fly anglers who are prepared to give advice on equipment, flies and opinions on the current best fishing locations. In addition to organizing trips to remote corners of the world, they can connect you with a qualified guide who will make your day on the water an event to remember. The gear available from Urban Anglers includes the best drawn from all of the major manufacturers to include Sage, Winston, Simms, Patagonia and many others.

The store is active in supporting local events and fishing organizations. You can find them at all of the major fishing shows that occur between January and April every Spring. In addition connecting at one of the shows, the store has an active website with fishing related news of interest to anglers in the Maryland and Virginia areas.

Store hours:

Monday	10AM - 6PM
Tuesday	10AM - 6PM
Wednesday	10AM - 6PM
Thursday	10AM - 7PM
Friday	10AM - 6PM
Saturday	10AM - 6PM
Sunday	Closed

The Albemarle Angler

The Albemarle Angler

1129 Emmet St.
Charlottesville, VA 22903
434 – 977 – 6882

Gordon English

Website
www.albemarleangler.com

The Albemarle Angler holds down the east side of the Blue Ridge. The operation is strategically located in Charlottesville where you can strike north or south into the trout water of the Shenandoah National Park as well as float or wade on the Shenandoah, Jackson, or James Rivers. Tucked next to the entrance to the University of Virginia, the fly shop serves as the headquarters for the guiding operation and offers a selection of the best gear from Orvis, Simms, Hardy, Fishpond, Sage and others.

In addition to providing advice and counsel on where to go and what to use, the Albemarle Angler has access to top-quality private water that includes Big Bend Farm, Hayfields Farm, Rose River Farm as well as Meadowlane on the Jackson. Beyond the private water, the territory covered by the guide operation is comprehensive and reasonably priced. If you are new to fly fishing, you can attend one of their Orvis endorsed fly fishing schools or even go on a guided trip that is specially packaged to cater to a beginning fly angler. The team is especially proud of their capabilities to handle multiple anglers on full day float trips for bass using their 15 foot raft that is built to withstand the beating offered by the rock ledges that hold the biggest fish.

Once you've experienced our great Virginia water, you may be interested in other top fishing locations. The store offers a worldwide fly fishing travel service in support of exotic locations. Give them a call for more information. The fly shop is open:

Monday through Wednesday between 9 AM and 8 PM
Thursday and Friday from 9 AM to 9 PM
Saturday from 9 AM to 8 PM
Sunday from 11 AM to 6 PM.

Water Flow

Culpeper - Average Water Flow in CFS (78 Year Average)

Day	Jan	Feb	Mar	Apr	May	Jun	Jul	Aug	Sep	Oct	Nov	Dec
	Mean of daily values for each day for 78 years of record in cubic feet per second											
1	667	570	703	879	548	499	327	309	255	383	354	592
2	626	646	654	856	608	470	383	283	222	469	388	624
3	676	701	658	840	613	592	338	261	231	349	418	493
4	635	793	791	773	590	543	324	318	246	276	587	655
5	596	758	894	869	638	598	323	315	316	298	628	612
6	592	664	838	802	744	497	313	258	692	671	473	525
7	579	733	876	765	648	511	281	246	827	453	453	521
8	614	741	789	757	729	434	310	232	396	413	526	541
9	731	588	779	776	663	396	293	326	406	456	451	500
10	621	596	701	843	602	500	285	284	312	414	489	550
11	571	592	708	734	559	480	295	306	288	314	418	771
12	605	658	802	701	605	436	277	273	273	267	487	592
13	553	696	808	829	622	498	295	388	363	305	562	556
14	705	879	820	751	617	471	294	289	346	341	469	578
15	639	826	816	776	554	424	297	298	298	546	472	538
16	615	642	743	853	576	377	339	360	273	731	390	543
17	530	704	807	942	563	406	299	401	443	384	402	553
18	542	803	927	777	567	483	276	718	401	424	372	536
19	707	777	875	655	579	518	234	628	597	471	382	491
20	739	709	1010	680	556	445	235	304	469	521	519	478
21	690	669	1090	623	590	464	282	255	363	447	447	589
22	681	750	913	705	541	918	285	246	404	357	447	579
23	685	839	881	667	520	491	293	274	392	428	460	491
24	685	760	841	658	449	365	343	278	314	431	412	490
25	762	789	807	687	459	310	268	319	332	393	462	508
26	808	834	776	1110	444	298	233	296	379	465	469	532
27	740	718	745	796	449	502	256	261	317	405	431	540
28	797	667	886	706	555	877	278	257	335	410	550	525
29	700	593	933	616	535	417	343	270	386	374	677	587
30	596		848	580	569	387	350	226	448	327	719	668
31	562		791		562		336	209		356		616

Culpeper - Average Water Flow in CFS (9 Year Average)

Day	Jan	Feb	Mar	Apr	May	Jun	Jul	Aug	Sep	Oct	Nov	Dec
Mean of daily mean values for each day for 9 years in cfs (1999-10-01 to 2009-09-30)											
1	659	343	472	679	535	299	287	202	184	369	271	734
2	866	395	668	1,080	550	282	249	177	363	319	247	606
3	630	416	687	924	644	271	564	145	414	271	232	516
4	555	485	565	705	508	487	436	257	273	233	222	466
5	508	457	636	630	461	793	398	208	283	212	256	445
6	497	686	636	570	440	453	445	159	323	341	620	465
7	460	774	574	563	400	657	347	194	239	667	405	441
8	502	515	561	577	390	543	532	161	185	1,230	566	413
9	488	433	564	648	786	415	367	132	695	834	444	408
10	449	400	508	627	589	354	278	176	346	395	358	568
11	432	387	475	670	542	331	259	270	242	318	352	1,530
12	427	385	458	674	764	380	231	361	203	297	778	951
13	400	384	438	853	509	365	301	457	258	264	1,050	693
14	1,340	471	435	800	433	332	298	228	239	235	583	738
15	656	529	414	865	404	586	274	173	228	299	468	658
16	516	432	537	819	567	431	231	163	201	235	522	695
17	458	467	688	669	518	531	197	155	186	239	805	980
18	469	504	509	622	629	563	198	135	582	243	638	771
19	527	459	458	615	716	486	200	152	2,170	208	576	613
20	584	413	891	569	629	632	217	134	1,250	199	667	575
21	491	454	1,700	656	567	512	239	125	461	194	492	535
22	426	1,020	1,110	742	559	500	231	116	364	192	484	495
23	454	1,470	831	871	634	396	231	103	902	192	632	575
24	414	771	742	659	510	323	199	96	514	174	543	721
25	403	617	625	617	450	279	169	92	423	203	573	630
26	363	552	564	635	481	287	169	156	468	269	501	680
27	363	523	534	627	430	285	180	189	357	448	460	575
28	340	516	875	608	419	746	155	133	634	478	561	511
29	323	357	769	662	395	441	214	192	1,290	397	681	485
30	327		1,040	551	352	332	265	229	458	358	1,470	463
31	333		781		315		243	175		323		437

Average Water Temperature

Culpeper Gage:

Day	Jan	Feb	Mar	Apr	May	Jun	Jul	Aug	Sep	Oct	Nov	Dec
	Mean of daily values for each day for 2 years of record in degrees Fahrenheit											

Day	Jan	Feb	Mar	Apr	May	Jun	Jul	Aug	Sep	Oct	Nov	Dec
1	43.0	33.1	41.5	54.1	66.7	78.8	77.4	80.8	77.0	66.7	54.1	48.6
2	41.9	36.0	43.0	56.8	69.4	79.5	76.5	82.2	75.9	64.0	54.1	55.0
3	38.8	37.0	45.0	56.7	65.3	76.1	75.9	82.0	76.5	64.9	52.2	49.1
4	37.8	37.9	46.8	55.4	63.3	74.3	77.5	81.5	78.3	67.3	48.9	41.9
5	39.6	38.5	46.9	55.8	62.1	74.5	76.8	81.7	78.4	67.1	47.5	39.0
6	43.5	40.5	45.5	54.1	61.2	74.8	77.4	81.3	77.5	63.7	48.4	37.0
7	45.1	41.7	43.9	51.3	61.0	74.8	78.8	82.6	76.5	64.8	46.8	37.0
8	46.4	40.3	43.5	49.8	61.3	77.9	80.2	83.1	77.5	74.1	46.0	37.4
9	46.2	39.6	43.5	50.5	64.2	79.3	80.8	82.4	77.4	74.8	49.8	37.0
10	43.5	38.8	44.2	53.1	69.1	77.7	80.8	80.2	77.0	67.6	50.5	38.3
11	42.3	36.5	47.5	55.9	72.1	78.8	79.7	79.2	75.4	64.8	50.5	40.5
12	42.3	34.7	48.7	58.3	72.7	79.9	80.2	78.6	73.6	63.0	51.6	42.4
13	42.8	34.3	49.8	53.6	71.4	79.9	79.7	79.3	74.3	60.8	52.0	43.5
14	44.6	37.9	52.3	54.0	68.4	79.7	79.7	78.8	75.4	57.7	54.3	44.1
15	45.1	36.0	54.9	50.5	68.7	77.5	80.4	77.7	75.6	56.5	54.0	43.2
16	44.4	37.4	52.5	48.4	70.2	76.5	80.4	78.3	71.8	56.8	52.5	42.3
17	40.1	37.2	47.8	48.2	69.3	69.4	80.6	79.2	69.3	64.2	51.3	41.0
18	37.2	38.7	47.1	52.0	65.5	69.3	82.0	78.6	68.9	66.4	47.1	40.5
19	37.4	38.7	47.5	52.9	62.8	70.9	81.7	78.4	68.9	68.7	48.2	41.2
20	36.7	38.1	50.5	54.0	64.9	70.5	82.4	77.5	68.0	66.7	48.0	39.7
21	34.2	38.1	51.1	57.0	67.8	72.1	81.3	75.2	68.2	60.8	48.2	39.4
22	33.6	39.6	50.4	60.3	68.9	73.9	80.2	74.1	71.1	58.8	53.8	41.2
23	35.1	39.7	52.2	63.1	70.5	75.4	78.4	74.3	72.1	59.4	49.6	43.5
24	35.1	39.2	53.8	65.1	71.4	75.7	77.9	77.4	69.1	58.5	44.6	43.5
25	35.1	39.4	53.8	65.7	73.0	76.5	77.5	79.3	68.0	55.2	44.6	41.9
26	34.0	39.6	54.3	64.2	74.8	77.7	79.2	77.0	68.4	53.6	46.6	41.5
27	34.5	40.5	55.6	62.8	75.0	79.5	80.8	74.1	70.2	54.1	49.1	42.8
28	36.3	40.5	56.8	63.1	75.6	80.4	80.1	73.6	70.9	54.7	46.8	41.2
29	36.3	38.1	56.3	63.5	75.2	80.2	81.3	73.6	69.1	53.2	46.8	41.7
30	37.0		54.1	64.6	76.3	79.3	81.9	75.6	67.6	51.8	47.7	41.9
31	35.4		52.5		77.5		81.1	77.7		52.0		42.3

Made in the USA
Charleston, SC
04 December 2010